"If you are a gifted kid; a gifted kid's mom or dad, teacher, or counselor; or if you even speak with a gifted kid occasionally—do yourself a big favor and read this book." —*Gifted Education Communicator*

"Excellent and clearly written. This book will help gifted children understand themselves and how to relate to others. I highly recommend it."
—James T. Webb, Ph.D., psychologist and author of *A Parent's Guide to Gifted Children*

"[A] well-organized, kid-friendly handbook that parents, educators, and anyone who works with children will also value." —*Youth Today*

THE SURVIVAL GUIDE FOR
Gifted Kids

For Ages **10** & Under
Revised & Updated 3rd Edition

Judy Galbraith, M.A.
Edited by Meg Bratsch, Illustrated by Nancy Meyers

free spirit
PUBLISHING®

Text copyright © 2013, 2009, 1999, 1984 by Judy Galbraith, M.A.
Illustrations copyright © 2013, 2009 by Free Spirit Publishing Inc.

The Survival Guide for Gifted Kids was originally published in 2009 as *The Gifted Kids' Survival Guide*.

All rights reserved under International and Pan-American Copyright Conventions. Unless otherwise noted, no part of this book may be reproduced, stored in a retrieval system, or transmitted in any form or by any means, electronic, mechanical, photocopying, or otherwise, without express written permission of the publisher, except for brief quotations or critical reviews. For more information, go to www.freespirit.com/permissions.

Free Spirit, Free Spirit Publishing, and associated logos are trademarks and/or registered trademarks of Free Spirit Publishing Inc. A complete listing of our logos and trademarks is available at www.freespirit.com.

Library of Congress has catalogued the previous version as follows:
Galbraith, Judy.
    The gifted kids' survival guide : for ages 10 & under / Judy Galbraith ; edited by Meg Bratsch ; illustrated by Nancy Meyers. — Rev. & updated 3rd ed.
        p. cm.
    Includes index.
    ISBN 978-1-57542-322-7
    1. Gifted children—Education (Elementary)—Juvenile literature. 2. Gifted children—Juvenile literature. I. Bratsch, Meg. II. Meyers, Nancy, 1961– ill. III. Title.
    LC3993.22.G35 2010
    371.95'72—dc22

                                                                                    2009000189

ISBN: 978-1-57542-448-4

Free Spirit Publishing does not have control over or assume responsibility for author or third-party websites and their content. At the time of this book's publication, all facts and figures cited within are the most current available. All telephone numbers, addresses, and website URLs are accurate and active; all publications, organizations, websites, and other resources exist as described in this book; and all have been verified as of August 2015. If you find an error or believe that a resource listed here is not as described, please contact Free Spirit Publishing. Parents, teachers, and other adults: We strongly urge you to monitor children's use of the Internet.

The names of the young people quoted throughout the book have been changed to protect their privacy.

Reading Level Grade 5; Interest Level Ages 10 & Under;
Fountas & Pinnell Guided Reading Level T

Edited by Meg Bratsch
Illustrated by Nancy Meyers
Cover and interior design by Michelle Lee Lagerroos

10 9 8 7 6 5 4 3
Printed in the United States of America
S18860915

Free Spirit Publishing Inc.
6325 Sandburg Road, Suite 100
Golden Valley, MN 55427-3629
(612) 338-2068
help4kids@freespirit.com
www.freespirit.com

**Printed on
recycled paper**

including 30%
post-consumer waste

Free Spirit Publishing is a member of the Green Press Initiative, and we're committed to printing our books on recycled paper containing a minimum of 30% post-consumer waste (PCW). For every ton of books printed on 30% PCW recycled paper, we save 5.1 trees, 2,100 gallons of water, 114 gallons of oil, 18 pounds of air pollution, 1,230 kilowatt hours of energy, and .9 cubic yards of landfill space. At Free Spirit it's our goal to nurture not only young people, but nature too!

green
press
INITIATIVE

Free Spirit offers competitive pricing.
Contact edsales@freespirit.com for pricing information on
multiple quantity purchases.

Dedication

To librarians everywhere who are terrific sources of information and book recommendations. When I was growing up, I spent many happy hours in the safe havens of libraries, and I felt supported by librarians who helped open the world of books to me.

To my mother . . . for giving me a good mind, and for raising me in a home where I was expected to use it well. I love books because of her, and I am ever grateful.

To my father . . . for teaching me to appreciate the wilderness (no matter how bad the weather), and for showing me the value of trying new things. I owe my adventuresome spirit to him.

Acknowledgments

One thousand students participated in the surveys for this book, and their responses were very important to its development. In addition, I'm grateful to all of the gifted young people who've written to me about their experiences growing up GT. Their letters telling me about their lives and the challenges, frustrations, and good things that go along with being GT are included within these pages. I'm especially appreciative of students' ideas, suggestions, and good humor. Hearing from readers always makes my day.

Many heartfelt thanks to Carla Valadez for meticulously tabulating the survey results for this third edition. Her efficient work and attention to detail was very much needed and appreciated.

I'd also like to thank the many parents and GT teachers who've contacted me over the years to let me know how kids in their care have benefited from *The Survival Guide for Gifted Kids*. Your words of encouragement and details about how you've used the book have helped to ensure the continuation of this "classic."

Last, but not least, I'd like to acknowledge my editor Meg Bratsch. Not only did she bring fine editing skills and creativity to this project, but her interest and enthusiasm made working on the book not like work at all. (Note to young readers: Meg was in GT classes when she grew up, so she's got firsthand experience just like you!) And special thanks go to designer Michelle Lee and illustrator Nancy Meyers. Your talents amaze me, and I appreciate all you've done to help this book be the best it can be.

Contents

Welcome to The Survival Guide for Gifted Kids

Dear Reader,

Did you know that kids like you chose the title for this book? Many simply said that "The Survival Guide for Gifted Kids" describes exactly what they need—information and ideas about how to survive and *thrive* in school, with peers, and at home. The book you're holding in your hands has answers you're looking for, plus new things to think about and ideas to consider. It won't answer all of your questions or solve all of your problems, and some of the experiences discussed might not be issues for you at all. But it is my hope that this guide—your guide—will help you make sense of some of the puzzling, amazing, and stressful challenges you face as a GT.*

GTs have told me that when they know more about giftedness, they feel better about themselves. And when you feel good about who you are, it's easier to *be* who you are and to make the most of your talents and abilities. This book was written for you, with the help of others just like you. Read it front to back, back to front, side to side, or skip around.

You might choose to begin by taking the GT survey on pages 114–116 (if you haven't already) to see how your responses compare with survey responses quoted throughout the book. Surveys were completed by kids in urban, suburban, and rural areas of the United States. Some kids had been in GT programs for several years, maybe even since first grade. Others were in a GT class for the first time. And still others had been identified as gifted, but weren't in a program yet because they switched schools and their new school didn't have GT classes. An equal number of boys and girls took the survey.

Some really good things have happened since I was a GT teacher, did my original GT surveys, and wrote my first survival guide for gifted kids in the early 1980s. Programs to support gifted students have become more established, more comprehensive, and more accepted in schools. (There wasn't even such a thing as a gifted program when I was in school!) This is partly why gifted kids complain less about teasing now than they did years

A theory called "The Flynn Effect" claims that the IQ (intelligence quotient) of the world's population is rising an average of 3 points every decade. If this is true, you are probably at least 8 IQ points *smarter* in certain ways than the kids who read my first book 25 years ago.

---

*Some gifted kids have said they don't like the label "gifted." Many prefer words like "smart," "intelligent," "accelerated," or "talented." I don't like labels either, but using "GT" in this book simplifies things. It stands for "Gifted and Talented," but you can decide what it means for you. Gargantuan Thinker? Gregarious Talker? Galactic Traveler? Good Thespian? Great Triathlete?

ago. Another big change is the Internet boom. Super-successful computer nerds with high IQs—like Larry Page and Sergey Brin (they founded Google) and Mitchell Baker (she launched the Mozilla Firefox browser)—and trendy technology companies—like The Geek Squad—have made it *cool* to be smart.

The National Association for Gifted Children (NAGC) estimates there are approximately 3 million gifted kids in kindergarten through twelfth grade in the United States. That's approximately 6 percent of the student population. So, while it sometimes might feel like you're the only one experiencing what it's like to be gifted, you're actually part of a pretty large group of people, including the nearly 1,000 kids who took my GT survey. The truth is: you're *not* alone.

About This Book

Throughout this book, watch for these repeating sections:

The **GTs Sound Off** sections contain actual quotes from kids who took the GT survey. See if you identify with some of the things these kids have to say.

The **Check It** boxes contain books, Web sites, and other places to check for more information.

The **Logophile** boxes include the meanings of words used in the book that you may or may not know. The dots between the letters indicate how the word is broken into syllables, so you know how to pronounce it.

> **Logophile**
> log·o·phile *noun:* a lover of words

The **Whiz Quiz** sections help you get to know your "inner GT" better and what it needs to thrive.

To jump-start learning about being GT, here's a short list of ways to succeed, no matter what your special talents and interests are. (It's also a sneak preview of topics covered in this book.)

5 Things GTs Need to Succeed

1. **Challenges.** Over and over gifted kids have told me they like to be challenged. In fact, many say it's harder for them to do simple things than it is to tackle difficult work. That means you need people, schoolwork, classes, activities, and opportunities that will S-T-R-E-T-C-H your mind.

2. **Self-esteem.** You need to feel pleased and proud of the person you are—*just the way you are.* This doesn't mean you can't or shouldn't try to be even better. But you need to believe in your own basic worth.

3. **Talk time.** You need opportunities to talk with people who respect and understand you. These people might be friends, family, or people at school or in your community. Let them know what you're thinking and how you're feeling. Ask them questions when you're confused, ask them for advice when you want it, and listen

Start a GT Journal

Writing in a journal is a great way to understand yourself better. It helps you organize your thinking and gives you the opportunity to express yourself whenever you need to. You might want to keep one as you read this book. Write your quiz answers, questions, opinions, ideas, frustrations, and joys about being GT. Decorate it, draw in it, doodle on it. Maybe even find a journal with a pocket where you can keep articles or pictures that you find related to giftedness.

closely to their feedback. The key is to find a few people you trust and talk with them regularly.

4. **Self-awareness.** You need to know yourself. What are your strengths and weaknesses? Your hopes and dreams? Who are you, anyway? If you're unsure, how can you learn more about yourself? One way to develop self-awareness is by asking yourself questions like these: What do I enjoy doing the most? How do I want to spend more of my time? What kind of person do I want to be? What do I think and feel, and why?

5. **Support.** You need trustworthy people in your life who are willing to help you. People you can turn to when the going gets tough. People who want the best for you. Make a list of people you can count on for help. Will you list your mom or dad? A brother or sister? Teachers? Friends? Coaches? Grandparents? Who else?

Finally, feel free to let me know what you think of the book when you're finished reading it. What was the most helpful, interesting, amusing, or encouraging? What insights would you add? You can write to me at:

Judy Galbraith
Free Spirit Publishing Inc.
6325 Sandburg Road, Suite 100
Golden Valley, MN 55427-3629

If you're online, you can email me: help4kids@freespirit.com

Or drop me a note at the Free Spirit Web site: www.freespirit.com

Judy Galbraith

P.S. I love getting letters from readers, and I *always* answer them!

Chapter 1

What It Means to Be Gifted

> "Being gifted means that I am smarter than my cat."
> —Rudy, age 9

4 Fast Facts About GT

FACT #1: *Gifted* means different things to different people.

If you're not exactly sure what *gifted* means, you're in good company. There are hundreds of different definitions of giftedness. Even the experts sometimes disagree with each other about what it means and how to identify it in people. "Who cares what it means?" you might ask. The answer: *you should care.* Knowing who you are is essential to getting what you want out of life and being happy. It's hard to be happy if you're feeling unsure of yourself or always wondering why you are the way you are.

Here's how some people and organizations have defined *giftedness.* See if you agree or disagree with these definitions:

The *Random House Dictionary* says...

gift·ed *adjective:*

1. having great special talent or ability: the debut of a *gifted* artist

2. having exceptionally high intelligence: *gifted* children

7

The U.S. Department of Education says...

"*Gifted learners are children and youth with outstanding talent who perform or show the potential for performing at remarkably high levels of accomplishment when compared with others of their age, experience, or environment.*"

> ### Logophile
> **po·ten·tial** *noun:* something that can develop or become actual

The National Association for Gifted Children says...

"*Gifted students give evidence of high achievement capability in areas such as intellectual, creative, artistic, or leadership capacity, and need services and activities not ordinarily provided by the school in order to fully develop those capabilities.*"

Professor Robert Sternberg says...

"*Giftedness derives from unusual ability to deal with novel kinds of tasks and situations.*"

Robert Sternberg has been a professor of psychology at both Yale and Tufts Universities. He believes that people with exceptional intelligence are especially good at clearly seeing and knowing how to adapt to their environments and also how to shape their environments to fit their needs.

> ### Logophile
> **en·vi·ron·ment** *noun:* the place or situation you are in

Dr. Barbara Clark says...

"*Giftedness identifies a level of brain development that allows rapid, in-depth understanding of complex ideas and operations, which may lead to outstanding creativity and performance.*"

Dr. Clark, a giftedness expert and former professor in Los Angeles, stresses the importance of a GT's interactions with his or her environment.

She says, "It is not possible for a brain to maintain its level of growth without help. It must constantly be challenged with new ideas, information, and experiences to continue to grow."

Dr. Joseph Renzulli says...

"*Gifted behavior occurs in certain people, at certain times, under certain circumstances.*"

Dr. Renzulli is the director of the National Research Center on the Gifted and Talented. He considers three factors important for the development of gifted behavior: above-average ability, creativity, and commitment to tasks. He believes that when someone shows all three factors combined, the person is showing giftedness.

The Columbus Group says...

"*Giftedness is asynchronous development in which advanced cognitive abilities and heightened intensity combine to create inner experiences and awareness that are qualitatively different from the norm.*"

The Columbus Group is a group of researchers who study giftedness. *Asynchronous development* basically means that your brain's moving very fast while your feelings and social skills are trying to keep up. This does not mean you are lagging behind emotionally or socially. Quite the opposite, you probably are more emotionally mature than other kids your age. It's just that thinking about complex issues and ideas might require a level of maturity far beyond your years.

Logophile

a·syn·chro·ny *noun:* the imbalance that exists when things occur at different times

Individual schools say...

"*Giftedness means that you do much better in school, and in less time, than many other students.*"

Some schools may define *gifted* by looking at levels of ability. For example, kids in the top 5 or 10 percent of their class in grade point average or achievement test scores may be those identified by the school as needing a more challenging curriculum.

Is your head spinning from all these descriptions of giftedness? Take a deep breath, because here's even more to think about.

FACT #2: There are many different ways of being gifted.

Academic ability.

Although few gifted kids are equally good at everything, many are gifted in one or more academic areas such as math, reading, writing, social studies, spelling, or science.

ASK YOURSELF: What classes seem to come naturally when you put your mind to work on them? You also probably enjoy these subjects the most. It's pretty difficult to be good at something you don't like!

Creative thinking. Highly creative kids are good at thinking up unusual ways to solve problems. They may have wild and crazy ways of doing things. They may be clever and good at thinking up jokes. Creative people are different, and they like it that way! (Sometimes adults have a hard time

ASK YOURSELF: Have you ever come up with a way to do your math problems that's faster than the way your teacher taught you? Are you sometimes able to get the right answers by solving the problems in your head? If so, when your teacher insists that you use the traditional problem-solving method and figure out the problems on paper, it might feel very frustrating and unnecessary to you.

accepting very creative kids, who often question why things are done the way they are. Creatively gifted people enjoy bending or breaking rules, and this can make some adults feel uneasy.)

Visual/Performing arts. Talented performers are considered gifted in a special way. They express themselves best through art, dance, drama, creative writing, or music. They're

ASK YOURSELF: Do you know anyone who fits this description? What's his or her special talent? Do you have a special talent?

often very imaginative and original, and they like to show their stuff.

Leadership. People with leadership ability are excellent decision makers. They like to take responsibility, and they have high expectations for themselves and others. They're often popular, self-confident, and good at motivating people.

ASK YOURSELF: Are you the kind of person who is organized and likes to inspire people to get things done?

General intellectual ability. Kids with this kind of giftedness are smart in many ways. They get excited about new ideas, learn quickly, usually have a large vocabulary, ask a lot of questions, and enjoy abstract, complex thinking.

ASK YOURSELF: Are you a superfast learner? Do kids ever think you're a show-off or a snob because you use big words? Do you know a lot about many different things? Do you often start projects on your own?

Psychomotor ability.
These kids have outstanding control of their motor (physical) abilities. They move their bodies with grace and coordination, perform intricate tasks with their hands, are good at navigating, and often show exceptional strength, speed, balance, and flexibility.

ASK YOURSELF: Do you love gym class? Do you learn new sports easily? Is being physically fit and strong appealing to you? Do you like dancing or gymnastics? Do you love to build things or do crafts? Do people always want you on their sports team?

FACT #3: Giftedness means different things in different cultures.

You might be considered gifted where you live because your abilities are valued and needed there. But imagine you are plopped into the middle of a jungle without any camping gear, fresh water, or matches. Would you have what it takes to survive *there?* An ability or trait that's valued in one part of the world may not mean much in another part. So, the criteria for giftedness vary from place to place, depending on what people value.

Now, you may *really* be confused. It's mind-boggling to think about the different ways people can be gifted—and I haven't even listed all the ways. You might feel frustrated trying to figure it all out. But keep in mind, there are no right or wrong answers to the question "What does *gifted* mean?" There are just different ways of talking and thinking about giftedness.

FACT #4: Most people DO agree about one thing when it comes to giftedness.

When you're gifted, you have high potential. When you have high potential, your brain, body, and spirit have the power to help you achieve great things *if you try.*

At some point in your life, your teachers or a parent might have said, "You're not working up to your potential." But what if you're doing all of your schoolwork, even finishing early? *And* you're getting good grades? *And* you're not goofing off in class?

GTs Sound Off!

What does *gifted* mean to you?

"To me it means I am the odd one out." —*Marisol, age 10*

"It means I never stop asking questions!" —*Devorah, age 9*

"I think it means I have a good chance of going far in life." —*Inga, age 10*

"It means not just knowing the answer, but thinking about why it's that way." —*Max, age 10*

"People expect more from me." —*Duncan, age 9*

"It means I'm smart enough to learn what Albert Einstein knew." —*Anthony, age 10*

"It means I have a special gift that came when I was born." —*Samir, age 7*

"It means I need to use my intelligence to help others and make the world a better place." —*Claire, age 9*

"It just means I have a faster rate of computing things in my brain." —*Nori, age 8*

"I am an independent thinker." —*Adriana, age 10*

"Being able to see things in a way others can't." —*Lexi, age 9*

What on earth are they talking about?!

The answer is: They know you're capable of more. Much more. You can go far beyond the regular schoolwork—or even the GT program—*if you try.* It's up to adults to give you opportunities, but it's up to you to take them, and to ask for them.

Maybe you've heard the old saying, "You can lead a horse to water, but you can't make it drink." If your teachers challenge you or your parent encourages you to explore new things—say "Yes!" (Unless you're already too busy to even take a drink of water, but that's another topic. See pages 93–94.)

You could be the smartest person in the world, but if you don't choose to use your high potential, you might as well have a brain the size of a toad (not that I have anything against toads).

> **"It is our choices, Harry, that show what we truly are, far more than our abilities."**
> —*Professor Albus Dumbledore,* Harry Potter and the Chamber of Secrets

Create Your Own Definition
What do *you* think *gifted* means? This might be a great thing to write about in your GT Journal.

G v. T

> **"I don't especially like the label 'gifted' because I think it sounds kind of bland and isn't very specific. I prefer 'talented.'"** —*Zach, age 10*

Is there a difference between being *gifted* and being *talented?* The short answer is: Not really. The long answer is: Traditionally, educators have used the terms to describe different things: *gifted* referred to high academic abilities, while *talented* meant superior abilities in the visual or performing arts. Even today, some school districts have separate programs for kids gifted in academics or in the arts. But current research shows that academically gifted students are often equally gifted in the arts, and vice versa.

For example, it's unlikely that you'd be super good at math without also having at least *some* exceptional ability in music, visual arts, drama, dance, or sports if you're given opportunities to develop it. That's a pretty good deal, huh? The only hitch is that some researchers claim artistic and physical talent can be easily "turned off" with lack of use. (Academic giftedness can be turned off, too, but not as quickly.) So keep up with that soccer practice and piano rehearsal!

The Many Sides of Intelligence

Gifted . . . talented . . . and wait, there's even more to the story! Why not dig even deeper to try to define *intelligence* itself? That's what Dr. Howard Gardner, a professor of psychology at the Harvard Graduate School of Education, has been doing for many years. His theory is called *multiple intelligences.* It suggests that the human brain contains at least eight different kinds of intelligence.* These include:

1. Verbal-linguistic intelligence (word smarts)
2. Logical-mathematical intelligence (number smarts)
3. Visual-spatial intelligence (picture smarts)
4. Musical-rhythmic intelligence (music smarts)
5. Bodily-kinesthetic intelligence (body smarts)
6. Interpersonal intelligence (people smarts)
7. Intrapersonal intelligence (self smarts)
8. Naturalist intelligence (nature smarts)

Every person—gifted or not—possesses all eight intelligences, and is usually strong in some and not-so-strong in others. Dr. Gardner's ideas have made many people think about how kids learn, and how teachers should teach.

---

*A ninth intelligence has been tentatively identified by Dr. Gardner. It is the existentialist intelligence and is strong in people who are good at placing things they learn into the vast picture of human existence. They ask big questions like "Why do I exist?" and "How do I think?" These people often pursue careers in philosophy, theology, or science.

WHIZ QUIZ:
What Are Your Strong Smarts?

Answer the following yes/no questions as honestly as possible.
Write your answers on a sheet of paper or in your journal.

1. I constantly have a song running through my head.

2. I am almost always reading something (book, magazine, Web site, cereal box, etc.).

3. I am drawn to bright colors and interesting designs.

4. I am good at crosswords, Scrabble, cryptograms, and other word games.

5. I am good at expressing my deepest feelings.

6. I can usually find my way around a new place pretty easily.

7. I can often sense the moods and feelings of others.

8. I enjoy solving difficult problems, especially with numbers (e.g., Sudoku).

9. I have pets and/or plants, and I like taking care of them.

10. I hear melodies and rhythms in the sounds around me.

11. I know my own strengths and weaknesses.

12. I learn best by doing things myself rather than watching others.

13. I like to examine and understand living things.

14. I make graphs, charts, and tables to explain things.

15. I enjoy telling and/or writing stories.

16. I like to work on group projects.

17. I love working on crafts and making things with my hands.

18. I try to be outside as much as possible.

19. I doodle when I'm listening in class or when I'm bored.

20. I'm almost always tapping a pencil, my foot, or my fingers.

21. I play many sports and am well coordinated.

22. I love trying to figure out how things work.

23. Most of my hobbies are ones I can do by myself.

24. My friends often ask me for advice.

Using the answer key at the bottom of this page, add up the number of A's, B's, C's, D's, E's, F's, G's, and H's you have, based on which of the questions above you answered "yes" to. For example, if you answered "yes" to question #1, you scored one A. If you answered "yes" to questions #2 and #4, you scored two G's, and so on.

Then, find the descriptions that match your scores to find out more information about your strong smarts and see some careers you might be well suited for. (Because you're GT, you're about 99 percent certain to fall into more than one category.)

Did you answer two or more . . .

A's? You have some mega music smarts. People with this kind of intelligence understand music, rhythms, patterns, tempos, and sounds. They easily hear tone and pitch, and they may be good at playing one or more musical instruments—with training or by ear. They often love many kinds of music.

> **Careers:** musician, conductor, songwriter, poet, DJ, composer, singer, or music teacher.

B's? You're plumb full of picture smarts. People with this kind of intelligence understand how objects and figures relate in three-dimensional space. For example, they can tell when a building isn't quite symmetrical.

They can judge the angle needed to score a goal in hockey or a basket in basketball. They can rotate complex forms in their heads and look at them from all sides. They're good at taking things apart and putting them back together, and they love games, puzzles, and maps.

Careers: painter, sculptor, filmmaker, video game designer, graphic artist, advertising executive, clothing designer, interior decorator, photojournalist, architect, construction worker, or machinist.

C's? You've got prime people smarts. People with this kind of intelligence are good at communicating with people and understanding their thoughts and feelings. They're natural leaders, caregivers, and mediators.

Careers: professor, teacher, principal, psychologist, counselor, salesperson, doctor, nurse, social worker, childcare specialist, politician, foreign diplomat, president, business owner, detective, law enforcer, or religious leader.

D's? You're brimming with body smarts. People with this kind of intelligence move their bodies with grace and ease. They enjoy training their bodies to be strong, flexible, and capable. They're good at handling and manipulating objects and tools, and they often excel at crafts—woodcarving, knitting, or pottery, for example. They can also be great mimics.

Careers: dancer, actor, surgeon, comedian, professional athlete, fitness instructor, coach, physical therapist, mechanic, or craftsperson.

E's? You're sporting some savvy self smarts. Folks with this kind of intelligence understand themselves very well—much better than others might understand them. They're acutely aware of their own feelings, dreams, and ideas. They set goals for themselves and reach them. They enjoy keeping journals. Often, those with self smarts also have people smarts, and are attracted to and successful in similar careers.

*See careers for **people smarts.***

F's? You have some noble nature smarts. People with this kind of intelligence feel a deep connection to the natural world of plants and animals. They love being outdoors. They're great gardeners and/or cooks. They understand the natural order of life and how living things fit into categories.

Careers: park ranger, biologist, botanist, zookeeper, chef, farmer, veterinarian, gardener, landscaper, commercial fisher, environmental activist, animal trainer, or florist.

G's? You've got some wicked word smarts. People with this kind of intelligence have an easy time using and understanding language. They may be great storytellers, and they enjoy reading, writing, talking, and learning new words (some are even logophiles!).

Careers: writer, editor, novelist, poet, public speaker, speechwriter, journalist, lawyer, researcher, publicist, or blogger.

H's? You're nimble with number smarts. People with this kind of intelligence are good with numbers and math concepts. They often enjoy science. They love games, riddles, and computers.

Careers: astronomer, physicist, engineer, crime scene investigator, pharmacist, chemist, analyst, statistician, accountant, computer programmer, software developer, meteorologist, or inventor.

Did you answer two or more for *all* (or almost all) the letters? Lucky you! You have what adults like to call *multipotentiality*. (Try saying that 10 times quickly. If you have no problem with this, you most definitely have word smarts.) Multipotentiality simply means that you have the ability to succeed in just about any endeavor or career you choose.

"I have word smarts and self smarts. I think I want to be an author when I grow up. I love reading and want to write a book of my own." —Brian, age 8

Dr. Gardner's theory of multiple intelligences doesn't explain everything about you, of course. But it can help explain why you might excel in one subject and struggle in others. For example, you may be really good at math and not so good at art, science, or reading. You might be a fabulous artist and a disaster when it comes to math. It depends on which intelligences you are naturally stronger in or have developed more. As for the others—the quiz questions you answered "yes" to *least* often—you have your whole life to work on developing those.

Mythbusters

One of the reasons GTs like being with each other is that they know what it's like to grow up gifted, so they don't have to deal with the false beliefs that many non-GTs have about them. What are these myths? Here are a few that *might* sound familiar . . .

Geeky Myths About Gifted Kids

Myth #1: Gifted kids look, dress, and act like geeks.

Oh, *really?*

Actually, many GTs look like anything *but* stereotypical geeks. In fact, some are among the most popular, stylish kids in school. And as for those GTs who *do* resemble geeks—in case you haven't noticed, geek is *chic*. Don't believe me? Check out the following list.

Logophile

chic (pronounced *sheek*) *adjective:* stylish

6 Celebs You Didn't Know Were Geeks

Nobody can argue that these celebrities are your typical nerds, geeks, and dorks! But all of them were GT kids once just like you and yes, they probably were teased for it.

1. Natalie Portman (actress) graduated high school with a 4.0 GPA, has a degree in psychology from Harvard, and is fluent in Hebrew, French, *and* Japanese.

2. Will Smith (singer, actor, producer) was offered a full scholarship to the engineering program at MIT but pursued a career in entertainment instead.

3. Alicia Keys (singer, pianist) graduated high school at age 16, was valedictorian of her class, and gave up a scholarship to Columbia University to pursue a music career.

4. Matt Damon (actor) was a straight-A student all through school and studied English at Harvard.

5. Frankie Muniz (former star of TV show *Malcolm in the Middle*) has a very high IQ and was teased in school for being smart . . . and short.

6. Shakira (singer) has a keen intellect (IQ is 140), wrote her first poem at age 4, and composed her first song at age 8.

"Geeks are supposed to be really smart and dress dorky. But you know what? I'm kind of proud of that. Even though I don't dress like a geek, I'm proud to be one." —Aja, age 10

Myth #2: Gifted kids don't need help in school.
Blarney! (as my Irish ancestors used to say)

All students need help in school, though the kind of help they need varies greatly depending on their learning levels.

Myth #3: It's bad for gifted kids to skip grades.
Hogwash!

Some people believe that if kids are accelerated (allowed to work ahead) or if they skip a grade so the schoolwork is the right level for them, it will be harmful to their well-being. This myth needs to be sent to the fourth dimension, because it holds kids back. Students who are allowed to work at their own pace usually like school a lot more than those who aren't, and they do better in school. This is true for kids who struggle as well as for gifted kids.

Myth #4: Gifted kids are gifted in everything and should always excel.
Nonsense!

Giftedness tends to center on one or two particular areas. Yes, there are those rare people who seem to be good at absolutely everything, but I bet if you asked them, even they would name some things they don't find easy to do. It's unfair to think that if you're gifted, you can't also be human and make mistakes, goof off, flub up, and be *un*gifted at times!

The truth of the matter: While giftedness is a complicated thing and there are many ways to define it, categorize it, understand it, and *mis*understand it . . . underneath it all, you're simply plain old wonderful YOU. There's no doubt about that.

Chapter 2

Life as a Gifted Kid: What's It Really Like?

"I feel like I'm watched every single waking moment of my life, and everyone expects me to be better than other people." —*Raj, age 10*

According to surveys, letters, and GTs I've talked to, here are the eight *worst* things and the eight *best* things about being gifted:

8 Great Gripes of GT Kids

1. We miss out on activities other kids get to do while we're in GT class.

2. We have to do extra work in school.

3. Other kids ask us for too much help.

4. The stuff we do in school is too easy and it's boring.

5. When we finish our schoolwork early, we often aren't allowed to work ahead.

6. Our friends and classmates don't always understand us, and they don't see all of our different sides.

7. Parents, teachers, and even our friends expect too much of us. We're supposed to get A's and do our best all the time.

8. Tests, tests, and more tests!

8 Big Benefits of Being GT

1. Our schoolwork in GT classes is more challenging and we learn more.

2. We get to do special things—activities, field trips, experiments, and projects.

3. Our regular schoolwork is easy for us to understand.

4. When we're in special programs and classes, we meet new people and get to be with friends who understand us.

5. We can help others with their work.

6. Our friends and other kids look up to us.

7. We look forward to a bright future.

8. Our GT classes are usually smaller than regular classes so we get extra attention.

Do you have gripes or benefits that aren't on these lists? Write them in your journal.

When Did You Know?

Some GTs know they're gifted soon after they start school (or even earlier). Their parents might have told them. Their teachers might have told them. Or they might have figured out for themselves that they aren't quite like many other kids their age.

> **"Most gifted children know they are different by the time they are five."** —*Dr. Philip Powell, psychology professor*

> **"I remember even in first grade I was totally obsessed with multiplication. And in second grade, I played fifth-grade math tic-tac-toe!"** —*Izzy, age 10*

> **"I never realized I was gifted until second grade and I made friends with smarter kids."** —*Elian, age 11*

Many GTs don't know they're gifted until they're accepted into a special program for the gifted and talented. Even then, some aren't sure, because often these programs aren't called "gifted programs." Why not? Because some adults aren't comfortable with that label. They worry that if kids are labeled "gifted," they might get conceited (they usually don't). Or that kids who aren't labeled "gifted" might feel bad (they usually don't, though they may have questions about where you're going, and why). So don't be fooled if your program is called something odd like ARC, GATE, PEGASUS, SAGE, ESPRIT, TAG, NEST, STEM, or QUEST. (Many of these are merely clever acronyms, such as TAG = **T**alented **A**nd **G**ifted.) No matter what they're called, these programs have the same purpose: *To challenge students who need more stimulation and a faster pace than the regular classes can offer.*

Most GTs who are selected for special programs are happy about it. They enjoy the challenge. They love learning new things. They like to learn at a faster pace with other kids who can keep up with them. Especially if they've been feeling bored and restless in regular classes, they're amazed to discover that learning is fun.

But they still have questions like:

* "How was I picked for this program?"
* "Why wasn't my friend picked? He/she gets good grades, too."
* "Does it mean I'm weird?"
* "Does it mean I should get straight A's all the time?"
* "Does it mean I can't ever make mistakes?"
* "What if the work is too hard?"
* "What if other kids make fun of me?"
* "How did I get this way?"

Adults don't always tell you what you want to know about being GT. They're afraid you might feel too different from other kids—at a time when most kids want to fit in.

But they're wrong.

When GTs find out about their giftedness, they usually feel GREAT!

Too Many Labels

Chances are you've always known that you think and learn differently from many kids. Your friends know it, too; that's why they say things like "You're so smart" or "You always get good grades."

But that's not enough. You want to know more. Being labeled "gifted," "talented," or "high potential" is a start. Labels are a pain, but they're part of life. They help us understand and communicate concepts and ideas. The problem is, when people can't agree on what the labels mean and which ones to use, kids (like you) may get stuck with *too many* labels.

If this happens to you, don't worry. Simply keep the labels that you like and that make you feel good, ignore the labels you don't like, and ask questions about the ones you don't understand.

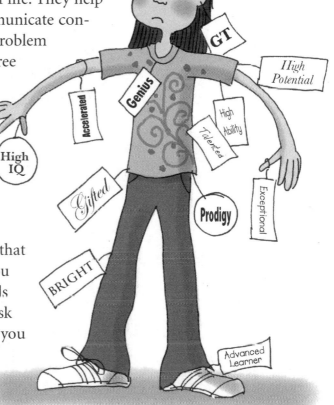

When you are labeled *gifted,* how does it make you feel? Write about it in your journal.

GTs Sound Off!

How do you feel about being called *gifted*?

"I don't like being called gifted. But high potential is okay." —*Julian, age 9*

"It makes me proud and want to try even harder in school." —*Tara, age 9*

"I feel like I can do anything." —*Liam, age 7*

"I love being called gifted. It's a compliment I will never grow tired of hearing." —*Luis, age 9*

"If it's an adult that says it I feel fine. If it's a kid, it's different." —*Suresh, age 8*

"It's okay. You get used to a lot of other worse names." —*Mei, age 10*

"I think everyone should be called gifted because everyone's good at something." —*Austin, age 9*

"It's just a title. It doesn't describe me." —*Jonathan, age 10*

"It feels great! I feel people know that I'm smarter than the average bear." —*Katie, age 10*

"Well, I'm kind of scared the word might get out. I would like it to be kept a secret." —*Basia, age 10*

"Sometimes I like it, other times I'm not in the mood." —*Ellen, age 8*

Chapter 3

YMIGT?

> **"Was I born smart or is it something I earned?"** —*Gillian, age 10*

Every GT has at least one pair of "designer" genes (for high intelligence, creativity, athletic skills, or leadership ability, for example). In other words, some of your giftedness is actually a *gift*—inherited from one or both of your parents, or perhaps a grandparent or other close relative. This means that features of your brain may be similar to those of one or more of your family members. Just like brown hair or blue eyes, gifted brains can run in families.

Meet Your GT Brain

"So my brain actually looks different from some other brains because I'm gifted?" you might ask. The answer is almost certainly: yes! Scientists have measured the brains of many different people and used MRI scans to record activity levels in particular areas of the brain. Their studies have shown a number of interesting things.

Logophile

MRI *noun:* MRI stands for magnetic resonance imaging, a medical procedure that uses radio waves to create computerized images of internal body tissues

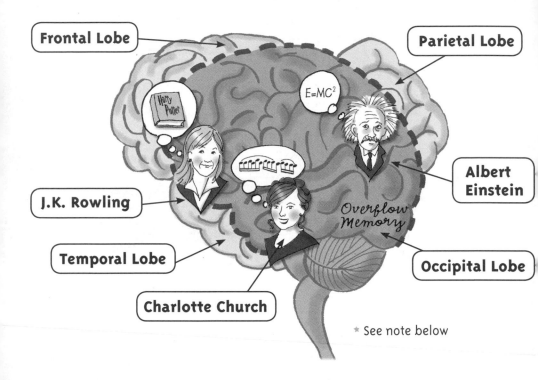

* See note below

Bigger Is Brighter (. . . *or* Is Brighter Bigger?)

There is a clear link between how intelligent you are (based on test scores) and how big your brain is. As a GT, you likely have more brain matter in your brain, especially in your *frontal lobe* (see diagram), which processes most general intellectual tasks. Of course, it's hard to know which came first: your big brain or your big IQ. In other words, did your big brain make you smart? Or did your smarts cause your brain to grow bigger over time?

> "Being gifted means having a big vocabulary and a big brain." —*Jonas, age 10*

One thing is certain: GTs' brains are wired differently from other people's brains. A brain is basically a jumble of about 100 billion electrical

---

*This diagram is for illustrative purposes only—your brain does not look exactly like this. The dotted line shows the outline of an average brain.

wires, called neurons, which "talk" to one another and make connections. And the more neural connections you have in a given area of your brain, the bigger that area will be.

For example, Albert Einstein's *parietal lobe* (see diagram), which is responsible for retrieving and processing math facts, was 15 percent larger than normal. Likewise, if you are gifted in music, like young opera star Charlotte Church, then your left *temporal lobe* (see diagram) is probably bigger than average. What if you're a gifted writer, like *Harry Potter* author J.K. Rowling? Then both your frontal lobe and left temporal lobe might be enlarged, because you've got tons of neurons chatting away in the two main language-processing centers located in those areas.

However, some areas of GTs' brains have also been found to have less brain activity and fewer neural connections than normal, a fact that has long confused scientists. The current theory is that gifted people's brains might simply build more efficient circuits in certain areas, so they are able to function better using less energy. Who knew that even your *brain* could be "energy efficient"?

Faster Is Brighter, Too

In addition to possibly inheriting a larger brain, you may also have inherited a faster brain. Genetics are a strong predictor of how fast a person develops neural connections. Evidence exists that your environment and your habits (like studying and practicing) can also help speed up these connections. Whatever the reason, your GT brain takes less time than average to turn new knowledge into routine knowledge—in other words, to learn.

Chances are that as a young child, and even as a baby, you were already showing signs of this faster learning speed. For example:

* When you were 2 months old you might have played with a rattle. A baby in the crib next to you at childcare may not have been able to do that for at least another month.

* When you were 1 year old, you might have already been walking up stairs. Your playmate down the block might not have been able to do that until he was a year and a half.

✦ And when you were 4, you might have been drawing realistic people with heads, necks, and hands, while some other kids in your preschool may not have done that until they were 6.

Loaded with Memory

If you think of your GT brain as a computer, you've now learned that it has a larger hard drive and a faster processor than most. Well, as it turns out, it *also* comes loaded with extra memory. When you're working on a complex problem-solving task, like a crossword puzzle or a math problem, your brain needs to store and retrieve lots of pieces of information from its memory bank.

In most people, this memory bank is only in the frontal lobe. But experiments show that in gifted people, the *occipital lobe* in the rear of the brain (see diagram) is also active during complex tasks, providing you with lots of space and power to quickly solve problems. This extra storage area also allows you to make more and faster connections between new things you learn. How cool is that?

Better Blood Flow & Communication

In addition to all of the electrical "juice," your GT brain also gets blood pumped into it—a *lot*. Your brain contains roughly 100,000 miles of blood vessels (enough to stretch almost halfway to the moon!) and recent MRI scans of the brains of kids highly gifted in math, for example, show *seven times* the normal blood flow to all parts of their brains active during math work. And finally, as if that weren't enough, the two halves of your brain (the right and left hemispheres) are likely best buds and communicate far better than average brain halves do. For this reason, many GTs tend to be at least somewhat ambidextrous.

> ### Logophile
> **am·bi·dex·trous** *adjective:* able to use both hands equally well; skillful

Using the latest technologies, neuroscientists (brain researchers) are constantly discovering fascinating new things about how people think, feel, and learn. In fact, it's possible that in the future, a person's intelligence will not be measured by IQ tests or college-entrance exams, but by a simple scan of her or his brain. A little freaky, huh?

Nature & Nurture

So certain brain features you've inherited are part of why you're gifted—but that's definitely not the whole story. Where you live, what you do, and everything and everyone around you also play a very important role. From the day you're born, your surroundings, your lifestyle, and your choices either build on or take away from your natural abilities.

You can think of your genes as forming the roots of a tree. As a GT, you likely have some very sturdy, healthy roots. But how big and healthy the branches and leaves grow depends on how well the tree (you) is cared for and nurtured. Do you live in a home where people value learning?

> "Healthy neurons are lush and bushy looking with lots of connections to other neurons." —*Dr. Nadia Webb, neuropsychologist*

NOT FEELING NURTURED? See page 76 for a list of people who might be able to help.

Do you eat healthy food and get enough sleep? Do you exercise? Do you try new things? Are you loved and supported? Just like a tree, you need nurturing from your environment in order to build on your roots.

Will I Always Be GT?

The "roots" of your giftedness will always be present, deep in your genetic code. But a lot depends on how others (like your dad or mom, teachers, and even friends) help or do not help you, and also on how *you* help or hinder yourself. For example, if you think to yourself, "I'm not that smart . . . I can't do this . . . I give up!" you're much less likely to build new neural "highways" and enhance the way your brain works. You'll be far more successful if you say, "I can handle this . . . I'm smart . . . I'll persist." (See the section on self-esteem, pages 64–65, for more details on this.)

You'll also ensure your smarts stay in tact by simply using them—*a lot*. In one experiment, scientists put volunteers through a brain "boot camp." They first gave them an intelligence test. Then, they gave the people a bunch of harder and harder memory tasks to do, such as solving puzzles. When the volunteers were retested, every single person increased their ability to reason, solve problems, and think more quickly. So, in some ways your brain is pretty simple: You either use it or lose it. And if you use it enough, there may be no limit to how smart you can get.

How Smart Do I Get When I'm Gifted?

Your brain processes around 400 billion bits of information every second (that's about equal to scanning more than *11,000 encyclopedia volumes in one second!*). But on average, you are only aware of roughly 2,000 of these bits—mostly concerned with your body (Am I cold? Hungry?), your environment (Where am I? Where am I going next?), and time (When is my assignment due? What time is my violin lesson?). However, scientists suggest that through intense observation, conscious choice, and creative thinking, it is possible to integrate more data. In fact, the human brain is *unlimited* in its potential for taking in information.

Check It!

Neuroscience for Kids

Explore your brain, spinal column, and entire nervous system. Learn about each layer of your brain, discover the differences between male and female brains, learn how chocolate affects your nervous system, and more! faculty.washington.edu/chudler/neurok.html

What If I Don't Want to Be GT—Can I Change?

> **"I don't want to be gifted. I am sick of it. Everybody bugs me and my parents are always trying to get me to do all these freaky gifted classes. It would be good to be normal for once."**
> —Keisha, age 10

Sure, you can change. (See "Whiz Quiz: Brain Boost *or* Brain Drain?" on pages 97–102.) But do you really want to?

Imagine you had a dog, Buddy, who loved to play fetch. The more challenging you made it for Buddy to fetch, the harder he ran to find whatever it was you threw. If it sometimes took Buddy a while to fetch, would you want him to give up? If Buddy wasn't always successful at finding the object you threw, would you stop playing fetch with him? Or if Buddy did fetch like a super-dog, and everyone at the dog park clapped and cheered . . . would you pull him away and put him back in his kennel? I bet you wouldn't. I bet you'd cheer on Buddy, too, and stick with him. So, why wouldn't you treat yourself as well as you'd treat Buddy? Why would *you* want to stop being all that you're capable of being and stop striving at the things you're interested in?

If you're really thinking you don't want to be gifted, things are probably happening around you that don't feel so good. Maybe some people in your life aren't treating you with understanding or respect. They may have unrealistic expectations of you that feel unfair. Or, they may think they always know what's best for you all the time instead of listening to what *you* want. Maybe what you really need is some help and encouragement. Lots of programs, classes, books, activities, and ideas have helped other GTs who, like you, were "sick of it all." Being GT can—and should—be an awesome experience, not a drag. Read on to see what steps you can take (and what steps other GTs have taken) to make this happen.

Chapter 4

GT Programs: What Works, What Doesn't, & What You Can Do About It

> "Finally! Once in a while I'm actually learning something." —*Stacia, age 9*

What Is a GT Program?

Programs or classes for gifted kids have lots of different names. No matter what the name, the basic goals are the same:

1. To provide you with challenges you aren't likely to get in your regular classroom, so you can learn at a higher level and stretch your mind.

2. To give you support and encouragement to do and be your best.

3. To place you in the company of other advanced learners, so you can support and challenge one another, and feel free to be yourself.

AIM
AIG
ARC
DELTA
GATE
PEAK
PEGASUS
REACH
SAGE
STAR
TAG
PACE
QUEST

Be As "In the Know" As Your Teacher

The ways schools organize offerings for gifted students have special terms. You might have heard your teacher or your parent talking about some of these terms. If you aren't sure what they mean, here's a short description of the most common ones.

* **Cluster grouping:** This is when a school clusters its gifted students together and places them into regular, mixed-ability classes at each grade level.

* **Compacted courses:** Some schools offer gifted kids alternate courses in a subject that compact, or condense, a large amount of learning into a shorter amount of time.

* **Continuous progress:** With this format, students progress according to their ability rather than their grade level.

* **Differentiated instruction:** Your teacher provides gifted students like you with different tasks and activities from the other kids in your class.

* **Enrichment:** When teachers help you study a curriculum subject in greater depth than usual, or you're encouraged to tackle subjects that aren't usually covered.

* **Grade skipping and subject acceleration:** When students skip one or more whole grades, or when they advance ahead to a higher grade level in a particular subject area.

* **Independent study:** Self-education. You get to pick your own subject, select your own resources, and create your own project under a teacher's supervision. (This is many GTs' dream!)

"As long as students are grouped by age in schools instead of by their level of knowledge or intellectual needs, identifying gifted kids will be necessary to ensure that the development of all children will *progress* rather than *regress*." —*Dr. Barbara Clark*

* **Magnet school:** These are schools that focus on a special interest area, such as a foreign language, the arts, or science and technology.

* **Pull-out program:** Students are pulled from their regular class for an hour or more each week for enriched learning opportunities.

Who Gets In?

Most of the time, teachers or other school officials identify kids for GT programs or classes. They often base their recommendations on test scores, teacher recommendations, and parent recommendations. They may also consider your achievements in school, including your grades.

What in the World Do Test Scores Mean?

Achievement Tests

Achievement test scores tell how well you're learning the things taught in school. The tests measure your progress in math, reading, science, social studies, and other school subjects. Your scores will probably be a little different in each area, because most GTs aren't equally good at everything. But if you're chosen for a GT program, it's likely that your scores are tops in more than one subject. In fact, many GTs' achievement test scores show them working in many subjects at least two years beyond where most kids their age are working.

IQ Tests

In some cases, a student may be given an intelligence test—an IQ test. IQ is the abbreviation for intelligence quotient. IQ tests measure how well you do on school-type intellectual tasks, but are not based directly on your school curriculum. If your IQ is high, you have the potential to do very well in school. (Whether you do is up to you).

The average IQ is 100. Anything over 100 is above average. Here's how other scores are classified—and about how many people have those scores:

IQ Score	Classification	About How Many People?
160	Very superior	1 in 10,000
150	Very superior	9 in 10,000
140	Very superior	7 in 1,000
130	Very superior	3 in 100
120	Superior	11 in 100
110	Bright	21 in 100

What IQ and achievement test scores don't show is how creative you are. Or what kind of athlete or musician or leader you could be. Or whether or not you have the motivation to use your GT brain. In fact, IQ tests have been debated for decades because of these limitations. Your GT program may not even bother with them. Some educators feel that assigning kids a number such as an IQ score does them more harm than good, since it is such a small part of a person's true intelligence.

Creativity Tests

Creativity is every bit as important as academic smarts in today's complex world. Because IQ and achievement tests don't do a good job of measuring creative thinking, kids are sometimes given separate creativity tests. These tests attempt to measure creativity by determining how well a person can come up with unique and imaginative solutions to problems.

WHIZ QUIZ:
20 Questions to Identify a GT

Answer the following yes/no questions as honestly as possible.
Write your answers on a sheet of paper or in your journal.

1. Are you able to concentrate on things for a long time?
2. Are you good at remembering details?
3. Do you enjoy observing things closely to try to understand them?
4. Is working with numbers easy for you?
5. When something interests you, do you really, really get into it?
6. Do you care about things being fair and "right"?
7. Do you have lots of varied interests?
8. Do you use many different and complex words when you talk and write?
9. Are you sensitive to how people treat you and each other?
10. Do you like thinking creatively, or "outside the box"?
11. Do you often try to get things perfect?
12. Do you have some friends who are older than you?
13. Are you generally good at solving problems?
14. Are you a whiz at putting puzzles together?
15. Do you have very vivid daydreams?
16. Do you feel compassion for other people and animals?
17. Do you have a keen sense of humor?
18. Did you start reading at a young age and/or do you read a lot now?
19. Do you often question what your teacher, parent, or other adult says?
20. Do you learn things quickly?

Teacher or Parent Recommendations

Did you answer "yes" to more than half of the questions? If so, that's probably a bigger reason than your test scores why you were chosen for your GT program. Schools often give teachers and parents a checklist similar to this one that tells them what to watch for. Students who have many of the qualities described in the checklist are likely candidates for GT programs. Teachers and parents also submit written recommendations if they feel a child could benefit from challenging classes. They write their perceptions and feelings about the students' abilities.

But even with letters, checklists, and test scores to help them decide who's GT, teachers and parents can still make mistakes.

Famous (& Infamous) GTs in School

Many famous GTs were misjudged, underestimated, or under-challenged when they were in school. You might be surprised to learn that:

* **Marie Curie** (Nobel Prize–winning scientist, first woman to earn a Ph.D. in science) was not allowed to attend college because she was female, so instead she attended secret science classes for women in people's homes.

* **Ludwig van Beethoven** (legendary classical music composer) had a music teacher who described him as "hopeless."

Check It!

Mensa
A score of 130 on the Stanford-Binet Intelligence Scale qualifies you for membership in Mensa, the International High IQ Society. Mensa members range in age from 4 to 94. There are preschoolers, high school dropouts, people with several Ph.D.s, and even big-name celebrities.
To find out more, visit the American Mensa Web site:
www.us.mensa.org

* **Susan B. Anthony** (leader of the U.S. women's suffrage movement that gave women the right to vote) learned to read and write at age 3. However, her teacher refused to teach her long division and other advanced topics because she was a girl. She was bored in school until her father withdrew her and taught her at home.

* **Rupert Grint** (actor who played Ron Weasley in the *Harry Potter* films) tried out for the first *Harry Potter* film after only acting in one school play. To everyone's surprise, he was chosen for the part. Unlike the others who auditioned, Rupert came in with hip-hop lyrics that promoted Ron Weasley.

* **Tori Amos** (Grammy Award–winning singer and pianist) at age 5 was the youngest person ever to be accepted to the prestigious Peabody Conservatory of Music. At age 11, she was kicked out for being "uncooperative."

* **Pablo Picasso** (often called the greatest painter of the 20th century) was so disinterested in school as a young boy that the only way his family got him to go was by letting him bring a live chicken to class so he could draw its portrait.

* **Walt Disney** (film producer, director, animator, and businessman) doodled and drew cartoons constantly in class. Even when he had no paper (his family was very poor), he drew on toilet paper.

* **Whoopi Goldberg** (Academy Award–winning actress) suffered from attention deficit hyperactivity disorder (ADHD) and severe dyslexia as a student and dropped out of high school at age 17.

* **John F. Kennedy** (35th U.S. President) received constant reports of "poor achievement" in school and was a lousy speller.

* **Agatha Christie** (renowned mystery novelist) said, "I was always recognized as the 'slow one' of the family." When she told her sister that she'd like to write detective stories, her sister replied, "They are very difficult to do. I bet you couldn't."

* **Albert Einstein** (Nobel Prize–winning physicist) performed so poorly in high school that a teacher asked him to drop out, saying, "You will never amount to anything, Einstein."

* **Michael Jordan** (Chicago Bulls basketball star) got beat out for North Carolina High School Player of the Year. His teachers told him to go into math "where the money is."

Who Might Get Left Out?

The selection process for GT programs doesn't always work the way it should. It isn't always fair. Some people who should get in are left out. Here are some examples:

Girls

Gifted girls can easily be overlooked in school, but not for the same reasons Marie Curie and Susan B. Anthony were. These days, the problem isn't sexism as much as it is self-esteem. Especially in middle school and high school, many GT girls hide their abilities so they can feel like they fit in with their peers and be "normal."

Boys with a Lot of Energy

Many young boys (and sometimes girls) have a tough time sitting still in class and doing paper-and-pencil work. Some are so energetic that they are wrongly believed to have a form of ADHD (attention deficit hyperactivity disorder).

Kids with Disabilities

Some kids have physical, emotional, or learning disabilities that make it hard to show their giftedness in "normal" ways. Research has found that when teachers and parent groups are asked to imagine a "gifted child," they almost never picture one with disabilities.

Kids Who Show Disruptive Behavior

Some teachers think that "good" behavior = GT and "bad" behavior = not GT. Musician Tori Amos, for example, lost her music scholarship because she spoke up about her dislike of reading sheet music and her interest in rock and pop music, which was not tolerated in the school.

Kids from Minority Cultures

Some tests are considered biased in favor of white students who are native speakers of English. Many tests appear to do a poor job of measuring the skills and abilities of kids from African-American, Latino, Native American, Asian, and other minority cultures, as well as from families where English is a second language. Also, the types of giftedness recognized in most GT programs are not the types that are valued in some minority cultures, and so those kids might not be motivated to join their school's GT program.

Kids from Low-Income Families

Many tests are also believed to be biased in favor of middle class and upper class students. In addition, kids whose families are struggling financially have a lot to worry about. Their gifts might get downplayed or ignored. And if they change schools a lot, or don't have a steady home, they're not likely to get into GT programs.

Kids Who Don't Do Well on Tests

Some GTs simply aren't good at taking tests. The test situation may be too stressful for them. Or they may have personal problems that keep them from concentrating. Either way, their scores don't show what they really know.

Kids Who Don't Get Good Grades in School

Some really smart kids might not be selected for GT programs because they don't get good grades. Grades don't necessarily have anything to do with giftedness. Some kids may not be interested in a particular subject, or they may not like school because it isn't challenging enough for them. They may not be motivated to do the work needed to get good grades. It's often these kids—the ones who are really smart but don't like school—who need GT classes the most.

Do You Fit Any of These Descriptions?

Maybe you or someone you know fits into one or more of the categories just listed. Are things in your life preventing you from being challenged as much as you could be in school? If this is the case, it's important that you talk to someone about it. Tell a teacher, school counselor, or parent about your concerns and ask them if you can be evaluated (or reevaluated in a different way) for your school's GT program.

How's Your Program?

If you're already in a GT program, how is it working for you? Does it help you enjoy school more? Is it fun and challenging? Are you getting enough support from your teacher to meet the challenges? Are there things you'd like to change about it? Read on to hear what GTs in the survey had to say about their programs.

GTs Sound Off!

What's rewarding about your GT program? What's frustrating about it?

"Our teacher pushes us to take risks, solve problems, and REALLY THINK." —*Uriel, age 11*

"When we learn something really new and tough, it's so cool to try and get it." —*Jacqueline, age 11*

"It is very challenging, and it's never boring." —*Matt, age 10*

"The people you are learning with are very smart and I always learn something new from them." —*Darien, age 10*

"We get to do projects that are fun and messy." —*Eilu, age 8*

"We don't get enough free time." —*Delena, age 9*

"It doesn't last long enough! I would have it ALL day every day." —*Cian, age 9*

"It would be nice for teachers to turn the speed dial down a bit (they talk way too fast)." —*Sara, age 10*

"Missing work in my other classroom. I fall behind sometimes." —*Violet, age 10*

"You can listen to other kids' opinions and you understand them." —*Aranza, age 10*

"They give us too much homework and it takes like five extra hours to do." —*Sabine, age 10*

Ways to Make Your GT Program Even Better

Some GT teachers get a lot of special training on how best to guide gifted kids. Some get very little. And some GT teachers don't get *any* help or training at all. That's why some GT classes aren't as good for you as others. If you wish your GT classes could be better, read on.

 According to the survey, here are the . . .

Top 8 Things Kids Would Change About Their GT Programs . . . and What to Do If You Feel the Same Way

1. **Classes would meet more often and last longer.** Think about it: You're gifted 24 hours a day, 7 days a week—not just a few hours a week. Let your teachers know the things you really like about your GT class, and why you'd like more time there. Get other GT kids who feel the same way to join you in talking to teachers about this. Ask if you can have more time in GT classes. Get your parents involved, too. If there's a GT parent group, ask your parent to be a member and to advocate for more offerings for gifted students.

> **Logophile**
>
> **ad·vo·cate *verb:* to speak or write in support of**

2. **Work would be more challenging.** Are you getting good grades even in your GT classes without having to try too hard? Do you start to snooze when you get what is supposed to be a "challenging" assignment? If so, that could mean you're not learning much that's new in ways that are interesting to you. Think about different ways you can learn about a subject that might be more meaningful. Set up a time to discuss options with your teachers. They won't always say yes to your requests, but if you don't try, you may never get what you need.

3. **There would be less homework.** Kids who go to GT classes shouldn't have to make up all the work they miss from the regular class, in addition to doing the work for their GT classes. That's

just *too much work*. Some kids say this feels like a punishment for being smart, and it's not fair. They're right. Talk to your regular class teacher and your GT teacher about your workload. Ask them if you can be relieved of having to do assignments that are MOTS.* Let them know how you feel, and see what compromises can be reached.

4. **We would have more free choice.** When GTs are asked what's the single thing they'd most like from teachers, they say: flexibility. They want more opportunities to work on projects that interest them, at their own pace, and in ways that fit their learning style. Ask your GT teacher if you can do an independent project or if you can do an assignment in a unique way.

5. **Meeting times would be changed so we don't miss our regular classes.** Sometimes gifted kids report missing out on fun things that happen in their regular class while they're in GT class. It may not be possible to schedule your GT class so that you don't miss any regular classes—there are only so many hours in the school day, and not all kids can come in early or stay late. However, you and your GT teacher can talk to your regular class teacher and ask him or her to try not to schedule special events on the days you're in GT class.

6. **We would read better books.** If you love to read—and chances are you do—you may feel frustrated with the books you're given to read, even in GT class. Ask your teacher what can be done so you have, at least some of the time, the opportunity to read books that really interest you. If you need recommendations for great books, ask your school librarian for suggestions (and check out the list on page 104).

7. **We would get more computer time.** If you really love working on the computer, ask your GT teacher what can be done so you have more computer time. Sometimes there are opportunities like this, but no one asks about it. Ask for what you want, and you're more

---

*More Of The Same, covering things you've already learned

likely to get it. Maybe your mom or dad can be a resource, too. They might be willing to buy you a laptop, or even give you their old one if they get a new one. Then, ask your GT teacher if you can bring the laptop to class to work on assignments.

8. **There would be no more tests!** Teachers are required by law to give standardized tests to all students at certain times during the school year. But your teachers get to choose how and when to test you on particular lesson units. These are the tests that you might talk to your GT (and regular) teacher about. Ask if he or she could hold contests or knowledge bowls instead of giving tests on some lessons. Competitions like spelling bees and math leagues can be a lot of fun, and they give students the chance to show what they know.

What If There's No GT Program?

More and more, often because of budget cuts, schools are eliminating programs for GTs. Parents who ask about gifted programs might be told, "All of our children are gifted." This sounds good, but don't believe it. All children are *not* gifted. It's kind of like saying "All of our children have 20/20 vision" when some, in fact, need glasses in order to see the board at the front of the classroom.

Even if your school doesn't have an official GT program, your teachers might be doing things to accommodate gifted students like you, such as giving you additional challenges and placing you in activity groups with other gifted kids. Chances are, your teachers are trying their best to provide you with learning opportunities that meet your needs.

However, they may *not* be trying their best. Or they may be trying, but not getting the support they need from the school. In some schools without GT programs:

* Gifted children aren't identified.

* Educators in the school district may not know much about giftedness, so they don't see the need for a program.

* Administrators (and some teachers) might not believe that gifted children truly exist as a special population, so they don't think GT classes are necessary.

* GTs are likely not getting the challenges and opportunities they need and deserve.

If your school doesn't have a GT program and your teachers are not meeting your needs as a gifted kid, or your school does have a program but it doesn't offer as much as you'd like, here are some things you can do:

1. Talk to your dad or mom. Ask your parent to join or form a GT parents group to advocate for more gifted education services.

2. Talk to teachers who believe that GTs should be challenged at school. Ask them what they can do to either help start a GT program, or to provide you and other GTs with more challenge and interest at school.

3. Talk with other GT students, and as a group set up a time to talk with school officials about changes you'd like to see in school.

4. Call, email, send a letter to, or even try to personally visit with your principal, the school board, your state representatives, senators, and the head of your state education department. Ask them to:

   * Put more funding for gifted education in their budgets.

   * Mandate gifted programs in your state's public schools, if there isn't already a mandate.

   * Require special coursework and state certification for GT teachers to ensure they know what's best for gifted kids.

While you may not be able to do much to change things by yourself, you do have the power to motivate adults who can. You probably know students in your school who get special help for learning challenges they face (maybe they have been diagnosed with ADHD, Asperger's Syndrome, or a learning disability, for example). Your school does a lot for these students. Your school should be doing just as much for *you*.

Chapter 5

When School Bores You Out of Your Brain

> **"I was so bored I finished reading a whole comic book series in class."** —*Elisha, age 9*

Boredom usually stems from not having enough interesting or challenging things to do. It also happens when you have to do the same thing over, and over, and over, and over, and over, and over, and over, and over.

One place where it should be easy to keep your brain engaged is in school. Sadly, for many GTs, too much of their time at school is frustrating and often a big bore. It would be unrealistic to expect that school *always* be challenging, interesting, and fun. But at least some hours of each school day should be meeting your needs, and *not* just in GT class.

The first and most important step toward making school cool— that is, more challenging and interesting—is to **know what you**

 According to the survey, here are the . . .

Top 10 Things GTs Do When They Finish Schoolwork Early

1. Read
2. Do other homework
3. Draw or doodle
4. Play games, do puzzles
5. Get on a computer
6. Write
7. Help the teacher or a classmate
8. Talk or text with friends
9. Sit and wait quietly
10. Sleep

ZZZZZZZ

btdt
been there
done that

"I feel bored in my regular class. I feel great in my GT class!"
—Hunter, age 10

need to keep your brain engaged. Nothing outrageous, just logical things like being able to:

* learn at your own speed, not someone else's
* test out of work you already know and understand
* study things you're interested in—beyond basic schoolwork
* work with ideas that really boggle your mind

The second thing you'll need to do is **help your teachers teach you better.** Remember that teachers have students of varying abilities in their classes: slow learners, fast learners, kids with learning differences and other special needs. If you want school to be cool for you, you can take the initiative. You don't have to stay stuck in the MOTS.* You can take some responsibility for your own education. Why not start today?

Logophile

in·i·tia·tive *noun:* **an introductory act or step**

*More Of The Same

GTs Sound Off!

How do you feel about working ahead in class?

"I feel like I have to always wait for the other kids to catch up. It can get boring."
—Sofi, age 9

"Being able to work ahead in class feels kind of like I'm free." —Noah, age 9

"I can't work ahead in class, but I can at home because the teachers don't live with me!"
—Delaney, age 8

"I feel like my teacher is holding me back by not letting me work ahead."
—Kele, age 10

"I usually don't work ahead, because then if you need help the teacher won't help you."
—Nadia, age 9

"I like doing things other kids don't know yet."
—Teagan, age 10

"I feel that instead I should be helping others do whatever they're doing."
—Quintin, age 10

"I feel like I am cheating if I work ahead."
—Karina, age 10

8 Great Ways to Make Regular School More Cool*

1. **Talk with your teacher about working ahead in class.** In their regular classes, many GTs have told me that a big issue is whether or not their teacher allows them to work ahead in the lesson, either in class when they finish their work early, or outside of class. If you'd like to work ahead, but your teacher won't allow it, try talking to him or her. Explain how you feel, and see if there might be room to compromise.

2. **Ask about skipping over work you already know.** This will free up time for more challenging projects. *Example:* Some kids take a pretest at the start of a spelling unit. If they score well on the pretest, say 95 percent or more correct, they don't have to work on learning the words for that unit, because their pretest score shows they already know them. You can apply this idea to other subjects, too.

3. **Become an expert on your favorite topics.** Talk with your teachers about working independently. This is a great way to study subjects in more depth than most regular classes allow. By working on your own thing, at your own speed, there's no limit to what you can learn. Ask your teacher or a parent to help you plan your study. Keep in mind that working independently doesn't necessarily mean working alone. GTs need help from others in learning the how-tos of independent study. Here are some questions to help guide you in creating an effective plan to present to your teacher:

   * *What will you study and how?* Be as specific as possible.

   * *Who can help you besides your teacher?* A librarian? Parent? A relative who is knowledgeable about your topic? Someone from your community?

   * *How long will your study take?*

---

*Talk with your mom or dad and ask for support. Tell her or him what's happening in school, and what's not happening for you. Share these eight ideas with your parent and see if she or he is willing to back you up.

* *How will you show what you've learned?* Talk with your teachers about creating unique displays for your classroom or school. You could work on them alone or with other students. You might design a new display each month, and take responsibility for putting it up and taking it down. Here are two examples of displays produced by GTs I've talked to:

Inventions display: Innovative GTs at one school participated in an inventors' fair and made a display to coincide with the event. They presented information about famous inventors and also about their own inventions.

Collections display: Collections make great displays, and most GTs I've known have created at least one. (The most unusual? One kid collected hundreds of different sugar packets from restaurants around the country!) Each display usually includes a brief description of the collection and information about how the collector became involved in the project.

ASK YOURSELF: If you could start a collection, what would you collect? How would you display your collection? What information would you provide about it?

---

4. **Talk with the teachers in your school who specialize in certain subjects**—those who teach art, music, dance, drama, creative writing, computers, and other subjects. Would they be willing to accept your help in planning activities and events or even lesson units? Could you be a computer aid, a tutor, or a cable TV operator? Volunteer to help them in creative and productive ways. Media centers and specialized teachers will likely welcome your skills and enthusiasm.

5. **Talk with your teachers and principal about starting mini-classes for subjects not taught in your school.** *Example:* If you'd like to learn a particular foreign language other than those offered,

such as Italian, find a few other students who share your interest. Tell your teachers and your principal about your idea. Ask them to help you figure out how, when, and where your Italian class could meet. They might also be able to help you find a tutor to guide the class. Borrow Italian language books and CD-ROMS or DVDs from the media center and you're on your way. *E' una buona idea!*

6. **Start a journal or blog.** Write your thoughts, poetry, stories, doodles, new ideas, or other creative jottings in a journal. Or, start a blog (short for "Web log"), which is like a journal, only it's published online. Post your musings whenever and about whatever you choose. You could blog about your favorite topics, pets, projects, and current events. Some people even blog about their daily breakfast cereals! See page 80 for a list of kid-friendly Web sites where you can create your own blog.

> **Important!**
> While blog sites for kids have strict safety measures in place to protect your privacy, your blog may still be visited by many people. So take care to post respectful content.

7. **Ask your teachers if you can demonstrate what you learn in new and unusual ways.** Instead of writing a report, how about one of these options?

   * Build a diorama (a 3-D miniature exhibit)
   * Write a play or short story
   * Prepare a speech
   * Compose a song or rap
   * Create a slide show or photo essay
   * Design a Web page
   * Construct a mobile
   * Record a video or podcast
   * What's your idea?

8. **Use your powers of persuasion to convince your teachers that you need an "anytime-of-the-day" library and media center pass.** Be a regular customer of your library and media center and learn as much as you can there—from books, encyclopedias, dictionaries, newspapers, magazines, reports, Web sites, podcasts, CDs, CD-ROMS, DVDs, computer programs, and anything else you can find. While teachers try to do their best, they're not going to be able to teach you everything you want to know.

> **"The next best thing to knowing something is knowing where to find it."** —*Samuel Johnson, 18th-century British author*

Find Other GTs & Take Action!

Have you heard other gifted kids complain about boredom, assignments, or tests? I bet you have. So don't just sit there—join together with these kids and brainstorm ways you can take action to change things. When brainstorming, remember these four rules:

1. Generate as many ideas as possible.

2. Do not criticize any ideas.

3. Do not discuss ideas until you are through brainstorming.

4. Welcome unusual ideas, no matter how zany or outrageous!

> ## Logophile
> **brain·storm *verb*:** to solve a problem by asking all the members of a group to gather together to come up with as many ideas as possible

What If You Hit a Roadblock?

What if you and your group suggest an idea and your teacher says no? Your teacher may not think it will work because such a thing has never been done before. She or he may be worried about how much time it would take, or that there isn't money in the budget for an idea like yours. So when you approach your teacher, it might help if you come prepared with answers to possible questions or comments like these.

As a GT, it's important to accept that grown-ups are human. Just like you, they make mistakes and don't always make the best decisions. They may say no to your ideas. But they're far more likely to say yes if you are cooperative, respectful, positive, and persistent. So keep trying! The truth is, if you never ask you'll never know what could have happened, and you'll never get to:

"YES!"

"Great idea!"

"Thanks for that suggestion."

"Let's do it!"

Chapter 6

Perfectionism & Other Pains in the Brain

> **"It seems that being gifted is tough, but I guess it is not as tough as going to war or trying to run a government."**
> —Louisa, age 10

Louisa is right. Growing up gifted probably isn't as tough as dealing with war or running a government, but sometimes it can still feel stressful, lonely, sad, and frustrating.

The Perfection Infection (& Cure)

It's been said by some experts that gifted kids are especially at risk for perfectionism. This could very well be true, since more than two out of three GTs surveyed said that their parents, teachers, and friends expect too much from them and think they should get A's and do their best all the time.

> **"I put a lot of pressure on myself, since last year all my grades were A's. I get really nervous about not being perfect."**
> —Deshaun, age 10

Logophile

per·fec·tion·ism *noun:* a tendency to feel that anything less than perfect is unacceptable

It's no wonder that nearly half of the kids surveyed also said they get nervous in school—I'd be a nervous wreck, too, if I thought I had to be perfect all the time! When kids suffer from perfectionism, they feel as though nothing they do is ever good enough. Not class assignments or projects. Not their performances in athletics, music, dance, or other things. They may even worry about how they look.

WHIZ QUIZ:
Are You a Perfectionist?

Answer the following yes/no questions as honestly as possible. Write your answers on a sheet of paper or in your journal.

1. Have you ever erased something on a paper so hard that you put a hole through the paper?

2. Do you begin assignments over and over, thinking your first try isn't good enough?

3. When you get papers back from your teacher, do you immediately examine any mistakes you made before noticing all of the correct answers?

4. Do you sometimes revise your assignments up until the very last second before handing them in?

5. Do you practice sports, dance, music, or other activities so much that you get exhausted or even sick?

6. If you get a B on a test or lose a sports game, does it ruin your whole day, and sometimes even your whole week?

7. Do you prefer to work on a project alone so that others can't mess it up?

8. Do you take a long time to make up your mind?

9. Are you always comparing yourself to others and coming up short?

10. Do you often criticize others when they make mistakes (even if you might not say it out loud)?

If you answered "yes" to more than a few of these questions, chances are you have a touch of the perfection infection. You probably sometimes . . .

* feel sad, lonely, or anxious (or all three)

* believe that nothing you do is ever good enough

* do things to please others instead of doing them because you want to

* don't try new things because you're scared you won't be able to do them perfectly

How did you get to be a perfectionist? You could have inherited genetic tendencies associated with perfectionism, such as anxiety and persistence. Or, others around you might have overly high expectations of you, saying things such as, "How come you didn't get an A?" or "You can do better than that."

No matter where your perfectionism comes from—your genes, other people's expectations, or your own expectations—it doesn't feel good. It can seriously hurt your ability to like yourself, be successful, and enjoy life.

What can you do if you're too hard on yourself? What can you do if others say things that leave you feeling like a failure? What can you do if perfectionism has you perfectly perturbed?

Tell yourself (as often and as loudly as you need to) . . .

> "I really *am* Mr. Perfect. If I'm not, my parents get mad at me." —*Finn, age 9*

The 3 Great Truths About Perfectionism

1. **No one in the world is perfect, and no one is good at everything.**
   Thomas Edison was one of history's greatest inventors, yet he didn't learn to read until he was 12. He certainly wasn't "Mr. Perfect." Instead of trying to be perfect in everything you do, learn to give the things that are most important to you your maximum energy. Then give yourself a break and don't go all out in everything else, or you'll end up exhausted and frustrated. When you take care of yourself in this way, you'll find you actually end up being super-successful in the things that truly matter to you, versus sort of successful in everything.

2. **It's perfectly okay to be imperfect!**
   People, often adults, will say it's okay to be imperfect, but they might also be sending you confusing messages. They might say it's fine to make mistakes, but then when you or someone else makes a mistake, they criticize or make fun of you. Never mind what other people say. Everyone, including you, learns much of what they know by making mistakes. You learn what to do differently next time. You are freer to take chances and try new things that also help you learn. Life is definitely more fun when you aren't afraid to flub up, goof, flop, bomb, and otherwise be *human.*

> "When I try too hard, I sometimes get so nervous that my brain doesn't work good and then I feel really miserable." —*Emma, age 8*

3. **Many, many things matter more than trying to be perfect.**
Getting A's in school might feel good, but they don't have anything to do with being a nice person or having a good life. It's important to spend your time and energy developing multiple characteristics that lead to success and happiness, not just perfect scores. Developing traits like trustworthiness, creativity, honesty, generosity, curiosity, and persistence make for a truly interesting, full, and admirable life.

> "I do the best I can, but getting perfect scores isn't everything in life. Lots of things are more important than that."
> —Trey, age 9

> "Perfectionism doesn't make you successful.
> *You* do—with your talent, your hard work, and your energy. Your perfectionism can only stand in the way of that by making you worry too much."
> —Dr. Tom Greenspon, psychologist and author

What's the Big Deal About Self-Esteem?

What does self-esteem mean, and why is it important? You've probably heard your teachers talk about it. In fact, many schools do activities to raise students' self-esteem and to help them build confidence. Some kids have said that they're sick of hearing about self-esteem because it's talked about so much in their school. It might be no surprise to you that being gifted doesn't necessarily mean you'll have any more or less self-esteem than other students. But whether yours is sky-high or down in the dumps, it's important that you know the truth about what self-esteem is, what it isn't, and why it's worth paying attention to.

Logophile

self·-es·teem *noun:* a realistic respect that you have for yourself; a feeling of self-pride

The key words in the definition of self-esteem are *realistic* and *respect*. Self-esteem doesn't mean bragging or exaggerating about who you are and what you can do. It means being realistic—honest—about who you are, inside and out. That includes knowing your strengths and knowing what things you need to work on. You might say, for example, "I'm a kind, smart, creative, and imaginative person, which helps me make friends easily and do great original work. But sometimes my imagination gets in the way of doing what I'm supposed to do on assignments or chores at home." Being honest about all parts of yourself makes it easier to accept and like yourself for who you really are, and not who you think you "should" be.

Respect is an important part of self-esteem, too. Without respect for yourself, you're less likely to feel comfortable standing up to teasers and bullies, or speaking up and asking for what you need or want at school, at home, or with friends. When you respect yourself, it might sound something like this: "I deserve to be challenged in school, and I'm going to keep asking my teachers for projects that are interesting to me. I know they won't always say yes, but I'm worth the effort to keep trying." When you have lots of self-esteem—or realistic respect for yourself— parents, teachers, classmates, and friends are more likely to respect you.

IMPORTANT: No one can give you self-esteem, and no one can take away your self-esteem. How much you have is up to you. So how do you build self-esteem? Do things that make you feel pleased with and proud of the person you are.

The Great (or Not-So-Great) Gender Gap

You've probably heard people talk about which is better, being a boy or a being a girl. But regardless of the different challenges boys and girls face, we need to see each other as people who want to be our best selves. That can't happen if we use stereotypes, myths, and old ways of thinking to define what boys can do versus what girls can do.

> **Logophile**
>
> **ster·e·o·type** *noun:* **a common idea about a type of person or thing, which is often not true in reality**

GT Girls

Years ago, many gifted girls were afraid to show their smarts. That's because most people believed that boys were naturally brighter, more able, and more ambitious than girls. They figured the girls would eventually get married and stay home with the kids, while the boys would eventually work and earn money to support them. So it didn't seem that important for girls to be challenged, to set high goals, and to succeed in school. If you were a girl in those days who wanted to get more education after high school, and go on to have a career, you probably would have only considered a few types of jobs, such as a secretary, nurse, or teacher.* Girls weren't encouraged to think about the many possibilities in life that were open to boys, like getting a Ph.D., becoming a doctor, starting a business, going to the moon, or running for president (just to name a few).

Today, thankfully, most people in North America and in many other (though not all) parts of the world agree: It's great for girls to be smart. Both girls and boys have the right to a good education. Both women and men have the right to equal work for equal pay. Even more important, both have the right to make choices about their lives. Women can work and have careers; men can stay home and take care of the children.

---

*These are all important jobs for both men and women today. But at one time, they were pretty much the *only* jobs for women. Thank goodness that's changed!

"Why are girls expected to play with certain things like makeup, and boys are expected to play with certain things like trucks? It's like someone is saying 'You have to play with this, and you have to play with that.' Why can't boys and girls just be allowed to do what they want without those expectations?" —*Jolene, age 10*

So as for those old myths . . .

Boys are smarter?
According to most estimations, U.S. author Marilyn vos Savant currently has the highest IQ score on record: 230. (The average IQ is 100.)

Boys are more able?
Russian gymnast Larissa Latynina has won more Olympic medals than anyone in history: 9 gold, 5 silver, and 4 bronze medals for a total of 18.

Boys are more ambitious?
The number of women-owned businesses is growing at twice the rate of all U.S. firms. About half of all privately held U.S. companies are owned by women—that's 10.6 million businesses that, together, generate nearly $2.5 trillion in sales.

Still, some girls try to hide that they're gifted, especially as they become teenagers. They may worry that boys won't like them if they use their brains. They may worry that other girls will think they're stuck-up or weird. They may worry that nobody will like them and they'll be all alone.

"There cannot be true democracy unless women's voices are heard. There cannot be true democracy unless women are given the opportunity to take responsibility for their own lives." *U.S. Secretary of State Hillary Rodham Clinton*

4 Frightening Facts About Females

* Up to 40% of girls begin dieting at age 10.

* Half of them say it's because of images in the media.

* By age 15, girls are twice as likely than boys to become depressed.

* Between 5th and 9th grade, gifted girls hide their accomplishments because they think that smarts aren't attractive.

Strong, self-confident girls become insecure about their feelings, abilities, and decisions. They focus on how they look and how boys see them, which keeps them from competing at school. Their view of the future—and what's possible for them—becomes more limited.

In short, their self-esteem often starts to fall.

Imagine that you're walking along a mountain path. You see a sign that says "WARNING! FALLING ROCKS!" What will you do? You'll be alert and watchful. You won't let a rock bonk you on the head.

You've just seen a sign that says "WARNING! FALLING SELF-ESTEEM!" What will you do? How will you protect yourself? By paying

Check It!

New Moon Girls

This magazine for girls, by girls, empowers them to pursue what they dream for themselves, not what society expects them to do. The Web site includes an online community forum, moderated by trained adults, where girls can discuss their dreams and emotions, and articles and opinions for parents and other adults.
newmoon.com

I Was Wondering . . .

Learn all about the accomplishments of contemporary women in science, and get an inside peek into varied and intriguing careers of some of today's most prominent female scientists.
www.iwaswondering.org

extra attention to your self-esteem when you are a teenager, and get help quickly if it starts to decline. (See page 76 for a list of people who might be able to help.)

GT Boys

Researchers have found that in regular classrooms:

* Boys call out answers eight times more often than girls.

* When boys call out answers, teachers are more likely to listen.

* When boys do not answer, teachers are more likely to encourage them to answer than they are to encourage girls to answer.

* Stereotyped male images still appear in textbooks, with many more male than female role models and authors studied in class.

So, it might seem like if you're a male student, you have it made. Think again. According to other studies:

* Most teachers prefer to be around girls than boys, and pay more attention to them in general.

* More boys than girls feel that teachers do not listen to what they have to say.

* By 12th grade, girls are four times more likely than boys to do their homework.

* Girls are more likely than boys to see themselves as college-bound.

As for giftedness, one study found that being GT is an advantage for elementary school girls but not for boys. Here are some possible reasons why:

Disobedience

Many schoolteachers tend to value conformity and obedience. Boys are more likely than girls to question authority, rebel, and be the class clowns or troublemakers.

> **"There comes a time in every rightly constructed boy's life that he has a raging desire to go somewhere and dig for hidden treasure."** —*Mark Twain, American novelist*

Sensitivity

There's pressure on boys to be macho—aggressive, competitive, and uncaring. Boys are taught to hide their feelings, not to show them. And they're never, ever supposed to cry. It used to be said that the least popular kid in America is the gifted, nonathletic boy. But that's changing thanks to some very famous "nerds" who've made it cooler than ever to be smart, like Bill Gates (founder of Microsoft), Steve Jobs (founder of Apple Computers), and U.S. President Barack Obama.

> "I used to be popular, but now I get teased a lot because I'm smart and because I'm not good at sports. I don't get why people won't accept me just as much for the things I'm good at. Why is being good at sports such a big deal as opposed to being smart?"
> —*Jacob, age 10*

> **ASK YOURSELF:** Are boys and girls treated differently in your school? If they are, what can you do about it? (*Tip:* You can start by treating the people you know—boys and girls—fairly and respectfully.)

Slower Development

Girls grow up faster than boys. In general, boys mature more slowly, especially in these three areas:

* Verbal and reading skills

* Fine motor skills (needed for writing and other intricate tasks)

* Concentration skills

Thus, bright, active boys might be labeled "hyperactive," "distractible," "sloppy," or "disorderly."

Check It!

Boys' Life: For All Boys

This jam-packed site accompanies *Boys' Life,* the magazine of the Boy Scouts of America. You'll find tips from the "Gear Guy" and the "Games Guru" as well as jokes, contests, widgets, videos, blogs, magic tricks, gym routines, and advice on serious stuff, too, like health issues and the environment. www.boyslife.org

Guys Read

A lot of boys (even GT boys) aren't too crazy about reading. This site was created to help boys choose what they read, pick from all different kinds of reading—not just school novels, and find out what other guys like to read. www.guysread.com

Because of these reasons, more young gifted boys than girls are overlooked for GT programs. And even in GT programs, boys sometimes have a disadvantage. If you're a gifted boy and you feel this way, talk to someone about it immediately. (See page 76 for a list of people who may be able to help.) You deserve to be understood and accepted for who you are, and challenged in ways that meet your needs.

What to Do When You're Freakishly Frantic or Down in the Dumps

Everyone has a bad day or a stressful week now and then. And sometimes, lousy feelings or tough times can last even longer. When this happens to you, there's plenty you can do about it.

Stress and Anxiety

"At night, I remember all the things I was supposed to do that day and if I've forgotten something, I get jittery."
—Rayen, age 9

"Just being around people I don't know makes me nervous until I get to know them."
—Kyle, age 8

No one—not kids, adults, animals, or even insects—can do very well in life if they have too much stress in their lives. And lots of gifted kids have told me that school is a major source of stress for them.

 According to the survey, here are the . . .

Top 10 Things GTs Stress About in School

1. Tests (especially timed ones)

2. Finishing their homework and the work they miss in regular classes

3. Grades (especially in math)

4. Performing in concerts and plays

5. Writing reports and essays

6. Speaking in front of the class

7. Being teased and bullied

8. Answering a question wrong in class

9. Making friends

10. Getting in trouble with their teachers

> What would you add to this list? Write in your journal about your "school stressors."

To be happy and successful in and out of school, you need to strike a balance between too little stress and too much. The key is to know where your balance level, or "zone," is, because everyone reacts to life's anxieties differently. Then, when you feel yourself getting over-stressed or under-stressed, you can take action to get back to your zone. For example, take a break from studying to talk with a friend. Take several deep breaths. Or listen to relaxing music.

Check It!

Be the Boss of Your Stress: Self-Care for Kids

by Timothy Culbert, M.D., and Rebecca Kajander, C.P.N.P., M.P.H. (Free Spirit Publishing, 2007). Discover how relaxation, positive thinking, good choices, and self-care skills can make you "the boss of your stress."

Behavioral & Learning Differences

Some kids are exceptional in more than one way, such as being identified as gifted and having LD (a learning disability), ADHD (attention deficit hyperac-

"I have ADHD and that makes it hard for me to concentrate, so kids sometimes say I shouldn't be in the gifted program." —*Sergio, age 9*

tivity disorder), Asperger's Syndrome, or other special needs. If you're one of these kids, you may have trouble interacting with people or have extra challenges in learning. This can be very confusing for you and the people around you. On one hand, you're really smart, while on the other hand, some of your traits and behaviors may not be typical for a gifted kid. People may not always "see" your gifts.

Another possibility is that people may not "see" that a gifted kid has a disorder such as ADHD, because her or his strengths and talents draw attention away from the disorder. These kids are praised for their abilities and yet must secretly struggle to maintain them because of their ADHD, without realizing why. This can lead to extreme frustration and poor self-esteem.

Meanwhile, a third possibility is that gifted kids who don't have learning or behavioral differences are labeled as having them, because some adults don't know much about giftedness. For example, they may confuse GT characteristics, such as being very intense or sensitive, as having Asperger's Syndrome. Or they might mistakenly label a GT with ADHD because he or she is simply bored in class and having a hard time sitting still and concentrating.

If you think you might fit into either of these camps—being extra-exceptional, struggling with a learning difference that has not been identified, or having your giftedness confused with something else—seek support from your dad or mom, teachers, or specialists in your school who can help you deal with these challenges.

Feeling Sad and Lonely

If you're naturally outgoing, or extraverted, you may find it pretty easy to make friends and find people you feel comfortable with. That doesn't mean you'll never feel lonely—all of us feel lonely sometimes—but loneliness is probably not a huge problem for you. However,

> "I sometimes feel like I'm all alone and it makes me sad."
> —Deondra, age 9

if you're a more introverted and private person (as many GTs tend to be) you may feel lonely more often. You might even feel sad or depressed, have negative thoughts about yourself, or be tempted to take drugs or alcohol to "fit in" or "ease the pain."

If you're feeling that way now, talk to an adult you trust right away. Let him or her know how you're feeling, and ask for help to come up with healthy ways to deal with sadness, loneliness, peer pressure, or feelings of insecurity. Also, read on for ways you can learn to make friends and connect with people.

Check It!

National Hopeline Network

800-442-HOPE (4673)
Call this 24-hour, 7-days-a-week, toll-free hotline for kids if you need to talk to someone right away about depression, suicide, drugs, physical or sexual abuse, or any other crisis you are experiencing.
Remember: You are never truly alone—there's always someone to help.

Adults Who Can Help

Here are some adults who might be good people to talk with about all of the issues discussed in this book.

* ✱ a parent, stepparent, or foster parent

* ✱ a grandparent, aunt, or uncle

* ✱ your friend's dad or mom

* ✱ a neighbor you know well

* ✱ a teacher

* ✱ a coach

* ✱ a counselor at school

* ✱ a professional psychologist

* ✱ a leader at your place of worship

* ✱ a youth group leader or after-school program leader

* ✱ an adult friend or mentor you know well

Chapter 7

Social Smarts

> "Lots of adults act as if we're 'emotionally challenged.'
> Like just because we're gifted, we don't know how
> to make friends. Also, they say that people should treat
> us normally, but they act like we're different and try to
> separate us from other kids." —*Javier, age 10*

What Are Friends & Where Do You Find Them?

Everyone needs friends—people to talk to and have fun with, and to share the ups and downs of life. We especially need at least a few people around us who like us just the way we are.

It's not always easy for GTs to find friends. No matter what you say or do, some people won't want to be friends with you. You can try and try and it won't make any difference. But guess what: This is true for everyone, not just GTs!

Maybe this is why some kids have an imaginary friend. (Do you?) Inventing a friend might be a way to practice talking with someone without having to worry about whether he or she likes you. An imaginary friend might also give you an opportunity to exercise your imagination and creativity. Or maybe you made up a friend because you're feeling

"A good friend is always there for you, not just in the good times."
—Maddy, age 9

lonely. If that's the case, it's very important for you to learn about how to make real friends, so keep reading!

In the survey, many GTs shared their ideas and thoughts on making friends and being a friend. Here's what they had to say.

✓ According to the survey, here are the . . .

10 Essential Qualities of a Good Friend

* Nice
* Helpful
* Trustworthy
* Understanding

* Funny
* Honest
* Encouraging
* Loyal

* Creative
* Smart

8 Great Friendship Tips from GTs Like You

1. Take turns being the leader.

2. Have your friends' backs. Always be there—not just in good times.

3. Let your friends do their own things. Don't boss them around.

4. Always be able to look your friends in the eyes. Be honest with them.

5. Listen to what your friends have to say.

6. It's okay for friends to fight sometimes. It means you're not afraid to disagree.

7. Laugh at your friends' jokes but never at their feelings.

8. Show your friends that you truly like them for who they are. Tell them the things you dig about them.

6 Tricks for Finding Friends

1. Volunteer. Volunteering is one of the best ways to build self-esteem and to meet people who share a common interest. It doesn't matter what you volunteer to do, as long as it is something that interests you. Are you tired of seeing litter? Join a group that has a cleanup effort in the parks in your neighborhood. Do you love animals? Find a way to help out your local animal shelter. Want to help make sure that people in your community have enough food to eat? Get involved in collecting food for a food shelf.

Roots & Shoots

With thousands of kids in nearly 100 countries, the Roots & Shoots network branches out across the globe, connecting youth of all ages who share a common desire to help make our world a better place.

Visit www.rootsandshoots.org to learn how you can get involved.

2. **Ask your parent to help you connect with other GTs.** Many parents of GTs are members of some kind of association devoted to meeting the needs of gifted kids. These groups often sponsor activities for kids. If your mom or dad isn't already a member of such a group, find out if there's one in your area to join. Talk with your parent about finding ways to meet other GT kids in and outside of your school.

3. **Join an online social networking group.** The Internet is full of sites that kids can join safely and freely to create a user profile, chat with others, create blogs, upload photos, listen to music, make trading cards, get help with homework, create and join interest groups, and tons more. Here are a few popular ones:

   * **Fanlala**
     www.fanlala.com

   * **Kidzworld**
     www.kidzworld.com

   * **Students of the World**
     www.studentsoftheworld.info

Check It!

International Telementor Program

Join this program to find a mentor at a university, organization, or business in your area of interest anywhere in the world, and communicate with him or her via phone, email, or letters. Who knows? You might even connect with a professor at MIT or the Sorbonne, or with an employee at NASA, Greenpeace, the Smithsonian, or even the Royal Shakespeare Company! Visit www.telementor.org.

4. **Get a mentor.** You don't always need to make friends with people your own age. A mentor is a caring adult who will spend time with you exploring your special interests. Mentors are encouraging people who like to be with kids, and who likely have a unique career or interest to share. You might find a mentor . . .

* in your neighborhood

* at school

* in your place of worship

* at a recreation center or community center

> **ASK YOURSELF:** If you could give one piece of advice to other GTs about making friends, what would it be? Would you (do you) follow your own advice?

* at your parent's workplace

* at a youth organization such as Big Brothers Big Sisters, the YMCA, the YWCA, Boy Scouts, Girl Scouts, Boys Clubs, or Girls, Inc.

* at a local professional organization (examples: staff members at a museum, media company, technology firm, research organization, or theater)

* at a local college or university

5. **Get involved in things outside of school.** Join groups, activities, classes, and clubs where you'll meet new people who share your interests.

6. **Don't limit yourself to only being friends with other GTs.** It's good to have friends who aren't in your GT program, too. It's a rare friend who shares *all* of your interests. Maybe you have a GT friend you play music with, someone else you play soccer with, and another friend you volunteer with at the local animal shelter. All of these friends can be equally important to you.

Friendship Fiascos & Fixes

No matter how close you are to a friend, there will be times when you don't get along. That's human nature and a part of human relationships. Gifted kids are generally really good at identifying the things that can go wrong with friends. And they're even better at coming up with solutions. Read the following to learn what other GTs say about friendship troubles and trouble-shooting, and see if any of these make sense to you.

 According to the survey, here are the . . .

Top 10 Troubles GTs Have with Their Friends

1. We like different things.

2. We compete about who is smarter.

3. We disagree about who is right about something (like game rules).

4. We get jealous of our friend's other friends.

5. We get mad when they don't share things with us.

6. We have a misunderstanding.

7. We fight over stupid things like playing on the computer.

8. We hate when they talk behind our backs and tell our secrets to others.

9. We get mad when they ignore or exclude us.

10. We fight over who goes first!

 And based on the survey, here are the . . .

Top 10 Ways GTs Problem-Solve with Their Friends

1. Take time away from each other to cool off.

2. Say, "I'm sorry" and hope they'll say it, too.

3. Try to talk it out and reach a compromise.

4. Find a way to laugh about it if you can.

5. Change the subject and see if the problem goes away.

6. Ask an adult for help.

7. Do something else you both like to do.

8. Play "rock, paper, scissors" to solve the problem.

9. Stay calm, take deep breaths, and just listen to the other person.

IO. Split the blame 50/50 and move on.

The Trouble with Teasing & How to Cope

Now that we've talked about making friends and being a friend . . . what about dealing with people who are downright *un*friendly?

According to the survey, a lot fewer kids get teased for being gifted and smart than when I wrote the first edition of this book 25 years ago. Still, if you're being teased or bullied, it doesn't feel good, it's not right, and there are things you can do to make the situation better.

Among the GTs who reported being teased, it is usually for doing well in school, and for being smart (like being smart is a *bad* thing?). For some GTs, teasing isn't a big problem. They're able to ignore it, shrug it off, and go on doing their thing. For other GTs, it's not so easy.

It may help to know some of the reasons why people might tease you. Here are a few possibilities:

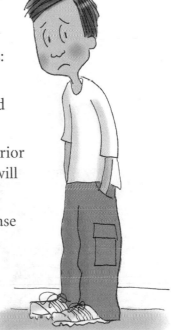

* They may be jealous of you. They may wish they could do as well as you in school or had your talents.

* They may have low self-esteem and feel inferior around you. Maybe they think teasing you will help them feel better about themselves.

* They may be giving into peer pressure to tease you, because others are doing it.

* They may tease just for fun. All kids get teased about something. If you weren't

GTs
Sound Off!

How do you get teased?

"I'm teased about how I think I'm better than everyone else, but I don't think that."
—Mercedes, age 9

"My program is called S.I.P. and kids say it stands for Stupid Immature People." —Jamal, age 10

"People say, 'You just got lucky. You aren't really that smart.'"
—Ryan, age 9

"People say I'm 'gifted' like I need help."
—Jackson, age 10

"I'm not usually teased. But some people say things in a good way, like, 'Hey, how was your trip to talented land?'" —Heath, age 10

"When I joke about silly things, someone says, 'And you're in GT?'"
—Megan, age 10

"If I answer a question wrong in class, they say 'I thought you were gifted!'"
—Danika, age 10

"I am teased about riding 'the small bus' in the morning."
—Bryn, age 9

"In 4th grade, I earned the nickname The Walking Talking Encyclopedia."
—Quan, age 10

"They say that I'm 'just too smart.'" —Grace, age 10

"Some kids ac like I'm an alien and that really hurts."
—Kai, age 8

being teased about being GT, you'd probably be teased about something else.

* If your friends are doing the teasing, it might be their odd way of showing you they like you. Some people aren't very good at giving compliments.

The next time someone teases you for being smart or doing something well, ask yourself the following questions. Then see if you feel better about the situation.

1. Who's doing the teasing? Is that person's opinion important to me?

2. Why are they teasing me? Just for fun? Because of peer pressure? Because they're jealous? Because they don't feel good about themselves? For some reason I'll never know? (You can't read another person's mind no matter how smart you are!)

3. Do I accept the teasing? Am I going to let it get me down or feel bad about myself? Or am I going to ignore it and do what I want and what I think is right for me?

4. Is this just teasing or is it bullying? For more about that, see page 87.

You can't control how you feel when you get teased—it's normal to feel sad, mad, embarrassed, or maybe even a little happy or proud—but you can control how you react to the teaser and to your feelings. For example, if the teasing hurts your feelings, are you going to say something mean back and then spend your time worrying that other kids don't like you? If so, you may never be able to do what you really want to do. You'll be too busy trying to please everyone else.

How Do Other GTs Deal with Teasing?

"When someone calls me weird, I simply say 'thank you.' If weird means smart, then I'm very, very weird!" —*Taylor, age 9*

"I usually respond by asking them a bizarre question, like 'Do you like fried chicken?' to throw them off guard." —*Dalton, age 8*

"I just think how they're going to work for me someday and ignore them and walk away." —*Judy, age 10*

If none of those ideas work for you, here's another technique for handling sticky situations:

1. Take a deep breath while counting to three. Then slowly breathe out while counting to six. (This will help you relax so you can talk without sounding too worked up.)

2. Stand straight and tall with both feet firmly on the ground.

3. Look the person in the eye and say how you feel about the teasing. Examples: "It makes me sad to hear that." "It makes me angry when people make fun of others." "That feels disrespectful to me." Resist the temptation to say something mean, or to tease back. That will only cause more problems.

4. Ask for what you want. For example, you might say, "Please stop saying that." "I'd like an apology from you, especially since I thought we were friends." "Quit it." "Your comment about me isn't funny. Please stop it."

By using your smarts, your words, your eyes, and your body language, you'll send a clear message: STOP THE TEASING. No one likes being teased, and by standing up for yourself you'll show kids what respect is about, and you'll be doing the right thing.

Will the other person stop? Maybe . . . and maybe not. You can't control what someone else thinks, says, or does. You can control what YOU think, say, and do. The important thing to remember is: You have a right to stick up for yourself and say what you feel.

What If the Teasing Becomes Bullying?

Bullying is when a stronger or more powerful person repeatedly and deliberately (on purpose) hurts or frightens a smaller or weaker person. Researchers who studied this problem found more than two-thirds of gifted students had experienced bullying by eighth grade. The most common types were:

* name-calling
* repeated teasing (either in person or using a cell phone or the Internet) about appearance, intelligence, and grades
* pushing and shoving

The study also showed that gifted kids are especially vulnerable to the effects of bullying, which can include low self-esteem, violent thoughts, severe anxiety, and serious depression.

If you're being bul-lied, it's very impor-tant for you to report it to an adult right away, such as a teacher, par-ent, or school counselor (see page 76 for a longer list of people who may be able to help). Becoming a bully yourself to get back at someone who's bully-ing you isn't going to help. In fact, if you start acting like a bully, things will be bad for you and everyone around you.

> "Sometimes, people will try to falsely be my friend just to get answers. Last year in school, I got kicked a lot, was called names, and someone slapped me on the back of the head."
> —Shane, age 10

You might be feeling sad or lonely if you're being bullied. You might even not want to go to school anymore. These are normal feelings all kids have when they're treated disrespectfully over a period of time. It takes courage to speak up. But that's the first step toward helping yourself. School should be a place where you feel safe, supported, and comfortable. Don't sit with those uncomfortable feelings. Talk to someone who can help make the situation better for you, and better for everyone.

By developing your social smarts, you'll find everything in life is just plain better. When you know how to reach out to people, make lasting friendships, solve squabbles, deal with meanies, and have fun with those around you who share your interests, you'll find yourself enjoying your days, yourself, and your gifts even more.

Check It!

My Secret Bully
by Trudy Ludwig (Tricycle Press, 2005). When Monica's friend Katie begins to call her names and humiliate her in front of other kids at school, she feels betrayed and isolated. But with help from her mother, Monica reclaims her confidence from a bully disguised as her friend.

Chapter 8

Family Frustrations, Family Fun

Most kids experience frustrations at home related to chores such as cleaning their rooms, taking out the trash, and not being allowed to play video games or watch TV as much as they'd like. GTs experience many home hassles, too, as they report in the following list. Which ones do you think most kids wish for, and which ones are more specific to gifted kids?

 According to the survey, here are the . . .

Top 10 Things GTs Wish Their Families Would Do Differently to Make Them Feel Happier

1. Listen to me more.

2. Stop expecting so much from me.

3. Don't yell at me when I don't do something perfect.

4. Be more excited and supportive when I get good grades and do good things.

5. Spend more time with me.

6. Let me play more and just be a normal kid.

7. Get more involved with my schoolwork.

8. Give me less stuff to do (chores, activities, lessons, etc.).

9. Stop fighting with each other.

10. Don't bug me when I'm trying to read/do my homework/play on the computer.

Great Expectations

> **"My parents expect too much of me. They think I am not human. They think I am superhuman."** —*Leah, age 9*

You may have guessed from the list that some of the biggest problems in particular for GTs are high—really, really high—expectations. What can you do when your parent pressures you to keep your room spotless, get straight A's, stop global warming, and create world peace? (After all, you *are* gifted, right?)

First, it might be helpful to understand *why* your parents want you to do so well at everything. Here are some possible reasons:

* When you do well, they feel good. They're proud of you and your accomplishments, and (rightly or wrongly) they may feel proud of themselves, too.

* When you do well, they think they look good in the eyes of people they know, such as your teacher and even their own parents. They may think that your accomplishments mean they're doing a wonderful job of being parents.

* Parents hear a lot about GTs needing to "work up to their high potential." Your parents may think that if you're not getting A's, you're not learning as much as you should and could. (However, you might be getting straight A's and *still* not be working up to your potential. How many times have you gotten an A and not learned much of anything new?)

* GTs sometimes act more grown-up than other kids their age. Parents get used to these grown-up ways, and they start to expect that behavior all the time. So if you act goofy, kooky, or just want to have some fun, your parents may think you're being irresponsible. (Now that's a silly idea. Especially because you are still a kid!)

Now that you know some reasons why parents have great expectations, here are some strategies you can try to improve the situation. After all, you're only human, right?

1. **Ask for a time to talk about it.** Pick a time when they have time (not as they're heading out the door for work, for example). Let them know how you feel. Angry? Stressed out? Unhappy? Inadequate? Pressured? Unloved? Like you'll never be good enough for them?

   Once your parents know how their expectations make you feel, they might be more likely to adjust their thinking, relax, try to encourage you, and accept you for who you are. If your parents aren't as understanding as you'd like, find another supportive adult—another relative, a teacher, a youth group leader, a school counselor, or one of your friend's parents. If things have been really frustrating you for a long time, you might suggest to your parents that you go together to see a family counselor.

2. **Let your parents know when you miss them, and when you want to spend more time with them.** Sometimes parents think kids are so busy with their activities or their friends that they may not realize you still want to be with them, too. Or, your parents may be so busy that they forget you still need them. Ask your mom or dad for a play date, or for homework help time, and then put it on the

calendar so you have that to look forward to. If you don't feel comfortable talking to your parents in person, leave them a special note.

3. **If you're being yelled at, it's important to try not to yell back.** Yelling doesn't help. In fact, it usually makes things worse. Later, when things have calmed down, talk to your parents about how it feels to be yelled at, and also how it feels when family members are yelling at each other. You might feel scared, worried, anxious, stressed, or all of the above. Ask them to try to talk in a regular voice. Let them know that you'll practice not yelling, too. If things don't get better, talk to another adult you trust. Let him or her know what's going on, and ask for help. (See page 76 for ideas of adults you can turn to.)

4. **Ask your mom or dad if you can take part in parent-teacher conferences.** That way, you can hear firsthand how your teacher thinks you're doing, and how your parent thinks you're doing. If what your parent and your teacher have to say differs from what you're experiencing, speak up. If things feel too pressured, or maybe not challenging enough, the parent-teacher conference is a great time to discuss ways to make things better for you, and to set new goals. You know *you* the best, so ask to be part of the conversation. *Tip:* Make sure your teacher knows you're coming to the conference so he or she is prepared.

> "My parents have my back, even if I get a bad grade. They don't yell. They just talk about what might have gone wrong." —*Eric, age 10*

When You're So Busy You Can't See Straight

"I always feel nervous on Wednesdays because I have regular homework, gifted homework, and soccer practice, so I'm up until about 10 at night!" —*Morgan, age 10*

Lots of gifted kids have many different interests and abilities. They're really good at some things and would like to be even better at others. If your parent encourages your participation in lots of activities, in and out of school, you might experience another thing common to GTs . . .

Doing TOO MUCH

You might have things to do every night of the week, and swimming lessons and dance rehearsal on Saturdays, and chores and homework on Sundays. HELP!!!!! When do you have time for yourself? If the answer is *never*, it's time to do something about your schedule. Here's how to start:

1. **Make a list of your commitments.** Include everything— homework, chores, extracurricular activities, lessons, practice, clubs, blog updates, etc., etc., etc.

2. **Prioritize your list.** Put a 1 by anything you *must* do—things that are not negotiable. (*Example:* You can't *not* do your homework or feed your dog.) Put a 2 by anything you *love* to do. Put a 3 by anything you think you can do without.

3. **Talk to your parent.** See how your mom or dad feels about your cutting out some of your commitments. Ask if you can give up at least a few of the things you marked with a 3.

4. **Try not to overbook yourself in the future.** Learn to really think about what you want to be involved in. If it's not really, really important to you, say no to it. All kids need time in their schedule for relaxation. Time to be free, to chill out, to have fun, to sleep, to daydream, to doodle, and to just hang out.

Siblings: Pests or Pals?

"My sister uses the fact that I'm gifted to call me witty names. Ironically, she is in a gifted program, too."
—Douglas, age 9

"My brother and sister say, 'Hey smarty pants, can you do my homework?'"
—Heidi, age 8

All brothers and sisters argue about things. It's natural, and it happens in every family.

But GTs run into double trouble when schoolwork is very easy for them and very hard for a brother or sister. Your siblings may be even unhappier if you're chosen for the GT program and they're not.

Try these tips for keeping the peace:

* Remember that each person in your family is special in some way. You won't all be good at the same things. Be sure to let your brothers and sisters know what you like and appreciate about them. Recognize their talents and tell them when they do something well.

* If your brothers or sisters tease you about being a brain or being in the GT program, it's probably because they wish they were, too. Think about how *you* would feel if they were selected for the program and you weren't. A little empathy goes a long way.

Logophile

em·pa·thy *noun:* the action of understanding, being aware of, and being sensitive to the feelings, thoughts, and experiences of another person

* Be patient. Try to understand that people learn in different ways and at different times. Your brothers or sisters may need more help and time to do things than you. They're not perfect. *You're* not perfect.

Some GTs have another sibling problem: The Super-Overachieving Big Brother or Sister. This is the person who did *everything* right, from getting straight A's to leading clubs to winning awards and elections. And now you're expected to follow in those giant-sized footsteps.

It's always best to just be yourself. If your parent compares you to your older SuperSibling, tell your dad or mom how it makes you feel (hopeless, frustrated, mad, sad). Ask your parent to please stop. If your teachers do the comparing, talk to them about it. Ask them to please see you as *you*, not as someone else's little brother or sister.

Some kids make the mistake of thinking that grown-ups are the only ones who can make family life better. Using the ideas in this section, you can see just how many ways you can help, too. You, and your family, are worth the effort.

"My parents don't admit it, but they expect me to be as smart as my gifted sister."
—Leo, age 7

GTs **Sound Off!**

What's the best thing your family does to help you feel loved, supported, and confident?

"They say even if I get an F minus, they'll still be proud of me." —*Maggie, age 8*

"My mom reads with me. My sister comforts me and talks to me about everything. My dad helps me with tests and studying. My brothers are fun. I feel safe and loved in my family." —*Brianna, age 10*

"My family helps keep me organized and tells me things that I can improve." —*Guillermo, age 10*

"They say, 'I love you' even when things stink." —*Joe, age 8*

"They always come to awards shows, sports games, and other things just to support me." —*Darsi, age 10*

"They answer all my weird questions." —*Sun, age 7*

"They let me do things in my own way at my own pace." —*Isaac, age 10*

"They give me challenging problems and do them with me." —*Jenni, age 9*

"They spend time with me and help me make the right choices." —*Steven, age 10*

"In the morning before school, my mom tells me, 'You can do it!'" —*Jack, age 9*

"My parents treat me the same as my siblings." —*Mariah, age 10*

Chapter 9

Great Brain Power

It's often been said, "A mind is a terrible thing to waste." And a brain (yours, in particular) is a terrible thing to drain. Your brain has *plasticity*, which means it will continue to produce new neurons throughout your life, that is if you stimulate, or "boost," it in the right ways. Otherwise, the neurons will "drain" away. How well do you take care of your brain? Take this quiz to test your brain-care IQ.

WHIZ QUIZ:
Brain Boost *or* Brain Drain?

For each activity, choose whether it's a brain boost (helps your brain) or a brain drain (hurts your brain).

	Brain Boost	Brain Drain
1. Play video games.		
2. Chat with a friend about your feelings, or write about them in a journal.		
3. Spend time each day updating your online profile or sending IMs to friends.		
4. Eat sugar and caffeine to pep you up.		
5. Watch a lot of TV.		
6. Try one of your friend's prescription pills to see if it might help you, too.		

	Brain Boost	Brain Drain
7. Dance around at home with your MP3 player.		
8. Stay up late doing your homework and get up early in the morning to work on it more.		
9. Take a break from studying for a test to play your guitar.		
10. Stay alone in your bedroom all day every weekend, reading books and listening to music.		

What's the Answer and Why?

1. **Brain Boost.** That's right: video games can actually be *good* for you. Because they are interactive, many video games help teach you how to strategize, recognize patterns, gather resources, make decisions, set goals, and use technology—all crucial skills you'll likely need in your future. Studies show video games can also help you increase your hand-eye coordination and develop your social smarts (especially if you have ADHD). Of course, just like any activity, gaming should be done in moderation. It should not replace interaction with real people *or* interfere with homework, chores, or other responsibilities. (See video game recommendations on page 106.)

> **Logophile**
> in·ter·ac·tive *adjective:* involving direct communication between a computerized device and the person using it

2. **Brain Boost.** Talking to someone you trust about your sadness, anger, or pain, or writing about your feelings in a journal can actually make the feelings less intense. This is because when you put feelings into words, you're activating a response in a calm part

of your brain (the *prefrontal cortex*) and reducing the response in your brain's "crisis center" (the *amygdala*). You're basically hitting the brakes on your emotional responses.

3. **Brain Boost.** A recent study of kids and their daily electronic communication habits found that, contrary to many parents' fears, chatting online and through text messages with friends is usually harmless. And it is becoming socially necessary. By participating in these activities (again, in moderation), you are gaining knowledge and skills you'll need to succeed in the future, such as: how to express yourself in writing, how to communicate with others, how to manage a public identity, and how to use technology. *Tip:* Offer to share your technical skills with your parents. They didn't grow up with the same technology and might not understand it very well.

4. **Brain Drain.** What you eat has a huge impact on how you think and feel. Eating or drinking things that have a lot of sugar, caffeine, or fat might make you feel good at first, but it's temporary. Your energy level will rise quickly and then crash quickly, too. The last thing you need while you're taking a test or working on an assignment is to fall asleep at your desk! If you want to take care of your brain, make sure the things you put into your body are healthy for you.

Check It!

Choose My Plate Blast Off Game

In this free interactive computer game, you can reach Planet Power by fueling your rocket with food and exercise. "Fuel tanks" for each food group help you keep track of how your choices fit into a healthy diet. www.choosemyplate.gov/games

5. **Brain Drain.** Watching television is often a brain drain, but it doesn't have to be. It all depends on what shows you watch and how much you watch them. Think about shows you learn from versus shows that are merely entertainment. It's okay to sometimes watch TV just for fun, but if most of what you watch is mindless, or if you're sitting in front of the tube eight hours a day, you're not helping yourself or your brain. Limit your TV watching, and talk to your parent, teachers, and friends to see what shows they think boost brainpower.

6. **Brain Drain.** It might be tempting to think that taking one of your friend's pills might make you feel good. After all, your friend takes them and seems to feel better, right? But drugs can have *very* different effects on people. For that reason, you should never take anything without your mom or dad's (and sometimes your doctor's) permission. You could seriously harm your brain and your body by taking a drug that isn't right for you. It is not worth the risk.

7. **Brain Boost.** Dancing is exercise, and exercise is a natural way to improve your mind and your mood. It gets extra oxygen flowing to every part of your body, which helps keep everything "breathing" and working well. (*Note:* your brain uses a full 20 percent of all the oxygen you breathe in, so exercise is especially good for it.)

Plus, listening to music while you're exercising can be an extra brain boost, since music also has beneficial effects on your brain.

8. **Brain Drain.** Do you think you need less sleep than others because you're gifted? If you said yes, you're wrong. Everyone needs an adequate amount of sleep to stay healthy, and that amount differs by age. Most adults need about 8 hours, but experts recommend that a kid your age gets at least 10 to 11 hours of sleep per night for your brain to perform its best. If that seems like a lot, keep in mind that your brain continues working and problem-solving even while you sleep.

$$if...$$
$$\left| \Psi(x) - \int_0^x \frac{dt}{\ln(t)} \right| < \frac{1}{8\pi} \sqrt{x} \ln(x)$$
$$then...$$

9. **Brain Boost.** Playing a musical instrument can not only boost your brain, but can also boost your test scores. A Harvard Medical School study showed that playing an instrument boosted kids' verbal scores by 15 percent, and nonverbal scores by 10 percent. The longer the musical training, the higher the scores.

10. **Brain Drain.** There's a lot to be said for spending time alone, doing your own thing—especially if that thing is a brain boost like reading or listening to music. But when you spend *too* much time alone, it becomes a brain drain. Some gifted kids who isolate say they just prefer to be alone, but it's probably also because they don't have a lot of skills at making friends. They are, in fact, lonely, which is different from wanting to have time to yourself. Being with people, especially those who you like and trust, enriches your life *and* your brain.

Witty Web Sites

The Internet offers endless brain-boosting opportunities. If you have access to a computer and the Internet, you have the whole world at your fingertips. Surfing the Web is great for building language, research, and technology skills. If you don't have a computer at home or at school, ask at your local library about free community Internet access. Of course, just like TV and video games, pay attention to how much time you're spending online and what kinds of sites you're visiting. Here are some good brain-boosting Web sites:

- **Google Earth**
  Download free software at this site that lets you fly anywhere on Earth to view satellite photos, maps, terrain, 3-D buildings, and even galaxies in the sky and canyons in the ocean.
  www.google.com/earth

* **BBC Human Body & Mind**
Click on "Interactive Body" to build a skeleton, stretch some muscles, organize the organs, and take the "senses challenge." Click on "Psychological Tests" to explore your memory and personality type, and find out what disgusts you and why.
www.bbc.co.uk/science/humanbody

* **Extra for Students**
Visit here for a thorough look at current world events. Find out how other kids feel about news items and post your own opinions in the "Student Voices" section.
www.pbs.org/newshour/extra

* **Olga's Gallery**
Visit one of the largest and most comprehensive art collections on the Internet. Browse over 10,000 high-quality photos of important works of art, as well as information about artists from all over the world.
www.abcgallery.com

* **National Geographic Kids**
Discover games, contests, polls, explorers' blogs, photos, stories, videos, activities, facts (about animals, people, and places), and *much* more at this award-winning kids' site.
www.kids.nationalgeographic.com

* **Make Beliefs Comix**
Design your own comic strips! Choose from 20 pre-drawn characters and dozens of facial expressions. Then, fill in text bubbles, and print or email your comic to friends.
www.makebeliefscomix.com

* **Kids on the Net**
Thousands of kids from all over the world have published their poems, stories, articles, reports, book reviews, and opinions on this site—and you can, too! Join in special writing projects, such as: Monster Motel, Kids' Castle, Spellbook, Dragonsville, and Adventure Island.
www.kidsonthenet.com

Brainy Books

I probably don't need to tell you that reading is a fantastic brain boost. No matter what form you read books in—from paper to electronic—they can be excellent sources of information, inspiration, fun, and learning. Here are some brilliant books with great GT-appeal:

* *The Star Pupil: A Dot's Quest to Find His Place in the World* by Carole Hamburger (Cherry Street Press, 2005). This is a tale of a dot's quest to find his special calling. After excelling in school, he travels to the four corners of the earth and encounters exciting opportunities that lead him to a surprising realization. Fiction, 32 pages.

* *Wonder Kids: The Remarkable Lives of Nine Child Prodigies* by Charis Cotter (Annick Press, 2008). Read the stories of how these gifted kids' amazing abilities were discovered and developed, and of how they used their gifts as they grew up. Nonfiction, 136 pages.

* *Millicent Min, Girl Genius* by Lisa Yee (Scholastic, 2004). Millicent Min is having a bad summer. Her fellow high school students hate her for being so smart, while fellow 11-year-olds hate her for going to high school. Then Millie meets Emily, and everything starts to change. Fiction, 272 pages.

* *Simon Bloom, The Gravity Keeper* by Michael Reisman (Dutton Juvenile, 2008). *The Teacher's Edition of Physics* is a special book—it can change the laws of physics and gives great power to the person who holds it. Eleven-year-old Simon Bloom ends up in possession of the book and must protect it from a mysterious woman who wants its power for herself. Fiction, 304 pages.

* *The Mysterious Benedict Society* by Trenton Lee Stewart (Little, Brown Young Readers, 2008). "Are you a gifted child looking for special opportunities?" When this peculiar ad appears in the newspaper, dozens of children enroll to take a series of mind-bending tests. But just four very special children succeed and embark on a secret mission that only the most intelligent and resourceful children could complete. Fiction, 512 pages.

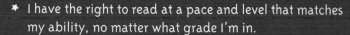

The Gifted Reader's Bill of Rights*

* I have the right to read at a pace and level that matches my ability, no matter what grade I'm in.

* I have the right to discuss what I read with my intellectual peers, regardless of their age.

* I have the right to reread many books and not finish every book I start.

* I have the right to use reading to explore new and challenging information and to grow intellectually.

* I have the right to read in-depth about topics of my own choosing.

* I have the right to learn advanced vocabulary and literary concepts.

* I have the right to be guided toward the best literature, rather than be told what I must read.

* I have the right to read several books at the same time.

* I have the right to discuss my reading choices with others, without having to defend those choices.

* I have the right to be excused from reading material that I've already learned.

Check It!

Reading Group Guides

Even better than reading books is talking with others about the books you read. So why not start a book club with your friends? Visit www.readinggroupguides.com for book club tips, guides, and title suggestions.

* Adapted with permission from Bertie Kingore, *Differentiation: Simplified, Realistic, and Effective* (Austin, TX: Professional Associates Publishing, 2004).

Vexing Video Games

While it's true video games can actually be good for you, keep in mind that this doesn't include *all* video games. Games that involve storytelling, solving puzzles, and creating things are far better for your brain than those that are mostly about shooting or racing. Here are games that are sure to challenge gifted minds. (*Note:* All have an ESRB Rating of "Everyone," so they are appropriate for kids.)

* *The World of Goo* (Brighter Minds, 2008, CD-ROM for Windows XP/Vista, Mac OS X). Drag and drop living, squirming, talking globs of goo to build structures, bridges, cannonballs, zeppelins, and giant tongues. An addicting and awe-inspiring puzzle game that will set you on an adventure you'll never forget.

* *Big Brain Academy* (Nintendo, 2006, Video Game for Nintendo DS). Fast-paced, challenging activities test your brainpower and improve your thinking abilities in areas like logic, memory, math, and analysis. Continuous display of your "brain weight" helps you track your progress during a match.

* *Bookworm Deluxe* (Mumbo Jumbo, 2006, CD-ROM for Windows 98/2000/XP). Link letters and create words to feed the hungry bookworm—but watch out for fiery red letters, because they'll burn down your library if you're not careful!

* *Chessmaster 10th Edition* (UBI Soft, 2004, CD-ROM for Windows 98/Me/XP). Includes 3-D animated chess sets and Chessmaster Academy classes designed to improve your game, regardless of your level of experience. A must-have for kids who'd like to learn or master history's greatest game.

* *Crazy Machines: The Wacky Contraptions Game* (Viva Media, 2001, CD-ROM for Windows XP, Mac OS X). Build your own unique contraptions while experimenting with gears, robots, explosives, and more. Put your machines to work to solve over 200 challenging puzzles.

Chapter 10

Freedom to Be GT

In this book, you've been reading what GTs say about growing up gifted, and about what you can do if things aren't going well for you in school, with friends, or at home. If you're worried or scared about trying to make changes for the better, you're not alone. Everyone gets a few butterflies in their stomachs when they think about making changes, or asking people for something to be different.

But you have the *right* to be happy and challenged and to reach for the stars.

Know Your Rights

How can you avoid being so nervous that you don't stick up for yourself and your rights? How can you communicate so you get what you need? To begin, it's helpful to know what your rights are! The National Association for Gifted Children has created the following "Gifted Children's Bill of Rights."

Gifted Children's Bill of Rights*

- ★ I have the right to know about my giftedness.
- ★ I have the right to learn something new every day.
- ★ I have the right to be passionate about my talent area without apologies.
- ★ I have the right to have an identity beyond my talent area.
- ★ I have the right to feel good about my accomplishments.
- ★ I have the right to make mistakes.
- ★ I have the right to seek guidance in the development of my talent.
- ★ I have the right to have multiple peer groups and a variety of friends.
- ★ I have the right to choose which of my talent areas I wish to pursue.
- ★ I have the right not to be gifted at everything.

Are there other rights that you'd like to have as a GT? Write them in your journal or make your own Gifted Kids' Bill of Rights poster to hang on your wall or in your locker at school.

---

*Reprinted with permission from the National Association of Gifted Children.

While none of these rights seems outrageous—and all of them make sense—many GTs sadly don't have them.

Get Your Rights

While you might wish for these rights, if you don't ask for them, it's not likely things are going to magically change. Your parent can help advocate for you, but you'll have the most success when *you* ask for things to be different, more interesting, better. When talking with your teachers or parent about things that concern you, keep these Do's and Don'ts in mind:

DO

1. Know what you want changed *before* you meet with your teachers or parent. Try to have as many details to justify your request as possible.

2. Try to think about the other person's position—and how he or she feels—so you can anticipate any possible objections.

3. Pick a good time and place for your meeting. (Obviously, if there are 15 kids standing in line to talk to your teacher or your parent is in the middle of a painting project, it's *not* the right time. Ask when would be a good time to talk.)

4. Start with a small request so you're more likely to succeed. Then work up to bigger requests once you've shown you can handle responsibility.

5. Be positive. If you have an attitude that's confident and cheerful, you'll be more likely to get a positive response.

Check It!

Search for
"Gifted Children's Bill of Rights"
to print a free poster of your rights:
www.nagc.org

Check It!

Stick Up for Yourself!
Every Kid's Guide to Personal Power and
Positive Self-Esteem by Gershen Kaufman, Ph.D.,
Lev Raphael, Ph.D., and Pamela Espeland (Free Spirit
Publishing, 1999). Learn how to stick up for yourself with
other kids, older siblings, parents, and teachers.

DON'T

1. Wait. You can start learning how to be assertive right now.

2. Blame people. It doesn't help. Instead, take responsibility and start by saying "I feel_____." "I need _____" or "I want _____."

3. Refuse to compromise. If you give a little, others are more likely to give, too.

4. Stop trying. If at first you don't succeed, try again . . . or try another way.

5. Be rude. Being unfriendly or using disrespectful language is, well, *rude.* Having good manners impresses people. Simply using the words *please* and *thank you* can have a huge impact.

> **Logophile**
> **as·ser·tive** *adjective:* displaying bold self-confidence in expressing one's opinion

A Few Final Words

> "It's not easy being green." —*Kermit the Frog*

It's not always easy being GT. But I hope this book makes it a little easier for you. Remember you're not alone, you have rights, and you can learn to stick up for yourself in ways that will make your life better.

I wish you a challenging, adventuresome, and free-spirited life.

GT Resources

Web Sites

Hoagies' Kids and Teens
Founded by a technology guru, writer, and mother of a gifted child, Hoagies' is the "all things gifted" site on the Internet. Go here for links to GT-friendly books, magazines, "nerd shirts," Web sites, movies, software, contests, and artwork and writing from GTs like you.
www.hoagiesgifted.org/hoagies_kids.htm

Contests & Competitions

Here are some contests to check out that are free and open to individuals in your age group. Check the sites for application instructions.

Davidson Fellows Scholarship Awards
These scholarships ($50,000, $25,000, and $10,000) are presented every year to extraordinary young people under the age of 18 who have completed a significant piece of work. Application categories are Mathematics, Science, Literature, Music, Technology, Philosophy, and Outside the Box. Davidson Fellows are honored every year in Washington, D.C., with Congressional meetings and a special reception.
www.davidsongifted.org/fellows

Do Something Awards
Athletes have the Olympics. Singers have the Grammys. World-changers have the Do Something Awards. Annual winners represent the best in their field or issue and are rewarded with a huge community grant, participation in a special award ceremony, media coverage, and continued support from Do Something. In 2008, the Do Something Awards became the first noncelebrity category of the Teen Choice Awards.
www.dosomething.org/awards

President's Environmental Youth Awards (PEYA)
Each year the PEYA program honors young Americans for finding creative ways of protecting our nation's air, water, land, and ecology. Past projects have included building nature trails, helping endangered animal species, starting recycling programs, and creating school yard habitats. All applicants will receive a signed certificate from the U.S. president, and winners will attend an award ceremony in Washington, D.C. www.epa.gov/education/peya (Click on the links at the right to download either a PDF or Word version of the application form.)

The Institute for Global Environmental Strategies (IGES) Art Contest
IGES's mission is to inspire the next generation of Earth and space scientists. This annual art contest is for students in grades 2–4. Each year's contest has a different theme; the theme for 2008 was "Trees: Making a World of Difference." The winning artist receives a $250 savings bond and his or her artwork is displayed on the IGES holiday card. www.strategies.org (Click on "Education" and then "Student Contests.")

National Geographic International Photography Contest for Kids
Enter a photo you've taken of something in one or more of the following categories: humor, animals, scenery, and people. The Canadian/U.S. grand prize winner from each category then competes against the National Geographic winners from around the world. *That* grand prize winner gets a trip to Washington, D.C. kids.nationalgeographic.com/kids/photo-contest

Young Playwrights Inc. (YPI) National Playwriting Competition
Have you written or ever wanted to write a play? YPI will give you a place to be heard. Winners will come to New York for the Young Playwrights Conference to work with famous theater artists. Your play might even be produced Off Broadway in the Young Playwrights Festival! youngplaywrights.org (Click on "Programs" and then "the National Playwriting Competition.")

GT Survey

Write your answers to the following questions on a piece of paper or in your journal.

About you . . .

1. I am a girl / boy (circle one).

2. I am _____ years old.

3. I have been in an enrichment/gifted program or class for _____ years.

About being a gifted kid . . .

4. What does gifted or high potential mean to you?

5. How do you feel about being called gifted or high potential?

6. Do you ever get teased about it?

7. If yes, how are you teased? What are you teased about?

8. Describe how you react when you get teased for being gifted.

9. What are your three favorite things about being gifted?

About school . . .

10. Are there things in school that make you worry or feel nervous?

11. If yes, what?

12. If you have questions about your own giftedness, do you know who to talk to?

13. If yes, do you talk to them?

14. If no, what would you want to talk about?

From *The Survival Guide for Gifted Kids: For Ages 10 & Under* by Judy Galbraith, copyright © 2013. Free Spirit Publishing Inc., Minneapolis, MN; 800-735-7323; www.freespirit.com. This page may be photocopied for individual use or use within a school or district. For all other uses, contact www.freespirit.com/company/permissions.cfm.

15. If you are in a program for gifted kids, what is the most interesting and challenging thing about your program?

16. Is there anything you would change about the program?

17. If yes, what?

For questions 18 and 19, choose one answer.

18. In school, the work I do is:

too easy   just about right   too hard

19. When do you usually finish your class work?

early   right on time   late

20. If you finish your work early in school, what does your teacher have you do?

21. What would you choose to do?

Choose an answer to complete this sentence.

22. My teacher encourages me to work . . .

at the same speed as others   at my own speed

23. Do you ever want to work ahead in class?

24. Are you allowed to work ahead?

25. How do you feel about working ahead during class? Outside of class?

About friends . . .

26. Describe a good friend. What is this person like?

27. What makes a good friendship?

28. What kinds of problems do you have with your friends?

29. What do you do when you have problems or conflicts with your friends?

From *The Survival Guide for Gifted Kids: For Ages 10 & Under* by Judy Galbraith, copyright © 2013. Free Spirit Publishing Inc., Minneapolis, MN; 800-735-7323; www.freespirit.com. This page may be photocopied for individual use or use within a school or district. For all other uses, contact www.freespirit.com/company/permissions.cfm.

About family . . .

30. Your family expects of you: (circle one)

too little   *about the right amount*   *too much*

31. What is the best thing your family does to help you feel loved and supported?

32. What is the best thing your family does to help you feel confident and successful?

33. Is there anything you wish your family would do differently to make you feel happy and comfortable?

Gripes . . . (gripes are things that annoy you)

Circle one answer for each of the following.

34. I miss out on some classes and activities that other kids get to do.

very true   *somewhat true*   *not true*

35. I have to do extra work in school.

very true   *somewhat true*   *not true*

36. I get teased for being smart.

very true   *somewhat true*   *not true*

37. Other kids ask me for too much help.

very true   *somewhat true*   *not true*

38. The stuff I do in school is too easy and too boring.

very true   *somewhat true*   *not true*

39. When I finish schoolwork early, I often can't work ahead.

very true   *somewhat true*   *not true*

40. My friends and classmates don't always understand me.

very true   *somewhat true*   *not true*

41. Parents, teachers, and even my friends expect too much of me. I'm supposed to get A's and do my best all the time.

very true   *somewhat true*   *not true*

42. Do you have any other comments about growing up gifted?

From *The Survival Guide for Gifted Kids: For Ages 10 & Under* by Judy Galbraith, copyright © 2013. Free Spirit Publishing Inc., Minneapolis, MN; 800-735-7323; www.freespirit.com. This page may be photocopied for individual use or use within a school or district. For all other uses, contact www.freespirit.com/company/permissions.cfm.

Sources for GT Facts

Chapter 3
Page 31: Information on the brain's energy efficiency from Dr. Richard Haier, University of California, Irvine, 2006.

Page 34: Some statistics on the brain's processing ability adapted from www.thebrainwizard.com.

Chapter 4
Page 41: Whiz Quiz adapted from "The Characteristics of Giftedness Scale" by Silver, Chitwood, and Waters, 1986. Numerous recent clinical studies continue to support these characteristics.

Chapter 6
Page 67: Statistics about women-owned businesses from The National Women's Business Council, 2007.

Page 68: "4 Frightening Facts About Females" adapted from the work of Anita Gurian, Ph.D., NYU Child Study Center, 2007.

Page 69: Facts about boys' and girls' treatment in classrooms from James Humphrey, *Stress Education for College Students* (Nova, 2003) and from "The War Against Boys" by Christina Hoff Sommers, *The Atlantic,* May 2000.

Chapter 7
Page 87: Statistics about bullying among gifted kids from a study by Jean Sunde Peterson and Karen E. Ray, Purdue University, 2006.

Chapter 9
Pages 98–99: Information about processing feelings based on a neuroimaging study led by Matthew D. Lieberman, UCLA, 2007.

Page 99: Information about the benefits of social networking based on a study by the MacArthur Foundation, "Living and Learning with New Media" led by Mizuko Ito, 2008.

Page 101: Recommended amounts of sleep from The National Sleep Foundation, 2004. Information about music and test scores from a study by Marie Forgeard, Ellen Winner, Andrea Norton, and Gottfried Schlaug, Harvard Medical School, 2008.

Index

A

Academic ability, 10
Achievement tests, 39, 40
Adapting, unusual ability for, 8
ADHD (attention deficit
    hyperactivity disorder)
    giftedness seen as, 45, 74–75
    GTs with, 43, 74–75
    programs for, 51
    video games and, 98
Adults
    acceptance of creative thinking,
      10–11
    as mentors, 80–81
    talking about feelings to, 75–76
    See also Parents; Teachers
Advocacy, 48, 51
Amos, Tori, 43, 45
Anthony, Susan B., 43
Anxiety, dealing with, 72–73, 93–94
Asperger's Syndrome, 74
Asynchronous development, 9
Athletic ability, 12, 15

B

Baker, Mitchell, 3
BBC Human Body & Mind (Web
    site), 103
Beethoven, Ludwig van, 42
Behavioral differences, 74–75
Benefits, 24–25
*Be the Boss of Your Stress: Self-Care
    for Kids* (Culbert and
    Kajander), 73
Big Brain Academy (video game), 106
Blogs, 57, 80
Body smarts, 18
Bookworm Deluxe (video game), 106
Boredom, overcoming, 52–59
Boys
    behavior of, 45, 70, 71
    development of, 71
    identification methods for
      gifted programs and, 72
    in regular school, 69–72
    stereotypes about, 67
    Web sites for, 71
Boys' Life (Web site), 71
Brain
    anatomy, 30–31, 32, 97
    blood flow in, 32

communication between halves
    of, 32
development, 8, 9
information processing ability
    of, 34
learning more about, 35
neural connections, 31–32, 97
quiz about boosts and drains,
    97–102
resources for boosting, 102–104,
    106
size and IQ, 30
Brain plasticity, 97
Brain scans, 29
Brainstorming, 58–59
Brin, Sergey, 3
Bullying, 87–88

C

Careers and types of intelligence,
    17–20
Challenges
    as focus of gifted programs, 26
    importance of, 4, 9, 34, 35–36
Chessmaster 10th Edition (video
    game), 106
Choices, 14
Choose My Plate Blast Off Game
    (Web site), 99
Christie, Agatha, 43
Church, Charlotte, 31
Clark, Barbara, 8–9, 38
Clinton, Hillary Rodham, 67
Cluster grouping, 38
Collections display, 56
Columbus Group, 9
Commitments, dealing with, 93–94
Compacted courses, 38
Computer nerds, 3
Computer time, 49–50
Continuous progress, 38
Cottler, Charis, 104
*Crazy Machines: The Wacky
    Contraptions Game* (video
    game), 106
Creative thinking, 10–11
Creativity
    as element of giftedness, 8, 9
    tests, 40

Crisis hotline, 75
Culbert, Timothy, 73
Curie, Marie, 42

D

Damon, Matt, 21
Davidson Fellows Scholarship
    Award, 112–113
Depression, 75, 87
Differentiated instruction, 38
Disabilities, kids with, 45, 74–75
Disney, Walt, 43
Disruptive behavior, kids who
    show, 45
Do Something Awards, 112–113
Drugs and alcohol, 75

E

Edison, Thomas, 63
Einstein, Albert, 31, 44
Empathy, 94–95
Enrichment, 38
Environment
    defined, 8
    importance of, 31, 34
Espeland, Pamela, 110
Expectations
    of others, 24, 67, 70, 89, 90–92
    perfectionism and, 60–61
Extra for Students (Web site), 103

F

Families
    expectations of, 90–92
    GTs' opinions about, 89, 96
    siblings, 94–95
Fanlala (Web site), 80
Feelings, dealing with, 75–76
The Flynn Effect, 2
Friends
    being good, 79, 82–83
    importance of, 77–78
    making, 79–81
    problems with, 82
    qualities of good, 78
Frustration
    ADHD and, 74
    causes of, 10
    families and, 89, 91–92

About the Author

Judy Galbraith, M.A., has a master's degree in guidance and counseling of the gifted. She has worked with and taught gifted children and teens, their parents, and their teachers for more than 30 years. In 1983, she started Free Spirit Publishing, which specializes in SELF-HELP FOR KIDS® and SELF-HELP FOR TEENS® books and other learning resources. She is the author or coauthor of numerous books, including *The Gifted Teen Survival Guide* and *When Gifted Kids Don't Have All the Answers* (with Jim Delisle).

Judy lives with her partner Gary in Minneapolis, along with their rescue dogs Twiggy and Violet, two spirited mixed terriers. Judy's hobbies include sailing, traveling, reading, scuba diving, biking, and hiking.

Judy can be reached at:
help4kids@freespirit.com
facebook.com/freespiritpublishing
@judyfreespirit on Twitter

Other Great Books from Free Spirit

Real Kids Real Stories Real Change

Courageous Actions Around the World
by Garth Sundem
foreword by
Bethany Hamilton

Thirty true stories profile kids who used their heads, their hearts, their courage, and sometimes their stubbornness to help others and do extraordinary things. As young readers meet these boys and girls from around the world, they may wonder, "What kind of hero lives inside of me?" Ages 9–13.

176 pp.; paperback; 2-color; illust.; 5¼" x 7½"

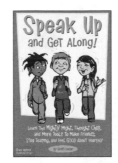

Speak Up and Get Along!

Learn the Mighty Might, Thought Chop, and More Tools to Make Friends, Stop Teasing, and Feel Good About Yourself
by Scott Cooper

This book presents 21 strategies kids can learn and use to express themselves, build relationships, end arguments and fights, halt bullying, and beat unhappy feelings. Each is clearly described, illustrated with examples, and accompanied by dialogue and lines kids can practice and try. Includes a Note to Adults. Ages 8–12.

128 pp.; paperback; 2-color; illust.; 6" x 9"

What to Do When Good Enough Isn't Good Enough

The Real Deal on Perfectionism: A Guide for Kids
by Thomas S. Greenspon, Ph.D.

This book helps kids understand what perfectionism is, how it hurts them, how to accept themselves as they are. Includes true-to-life vignettes, exercises, and a note to parents. Ages 9–13.

144 pp.; paperback; 2-color; illust.; 5⅜" x 8⅜"

You're Smarter Than You Think

A Kid's Guide to Multiple Intelligences (Revised & Updated Edition)
by Thomas Armstrong, Ph.D.

Written by an award-winning expert on multiple intelligences, this book introduces the theory, explains the different types of intelligences (like Word Smart, Self Smart, Body Smart), and helps kids identify their own learning strengths and use their special skills at school, at home, and in life. Ages 9–14.

208 pp.; paperback; 2-color; illust.; 7" x 9"

Find all the Free Spirit SURVIVAL GUIDES for Kids at www.freespirit.com/survival-guides-for-kids

Interested in purchasing multiple quantities and receiving volume discounts? Contact edsales@freespirit.com or call 1.800.735.7323 and ask for Education Sales.

Many Free Spirit authors are available for speaking engagements, workshops, and keynotes. Contact speakers@freespirit.com or call 1.800.735.7323.

For pricing information, to place an order, or to request a free catalog, contact:

Free Spirit Publishing Inc.
6325 Sandburg Road • Suite 100 • Golden Valley, MN 55427-3629
toll-free 800.735.7323 • local 612.338.2068 • fax 612.337.5050
help4kids@freespirit.com • www.freespirit.com